Bulletin
of the European Union

Supplement 9/97

Commission opinion
on Slovakia's application
for membership
of the European Union

Document drawn up on the basis of COM(97) 2004 final

European Commission

ZZ
EM115
97B09

A great deal of additional information on the European Union is available on the Internet.
It can be accessed through the Europa server (http://europa.eu.int)

Cataloguing data can be found at the end of this publication

Luxembourg: Office for Official Publications of the European Communities, 1997

ISBN 92-828-1248-0

Printed in Germany

PRINTED ON WHITE CHLORINE-FREE PAPER

CORRIGENDA

Supplement 9/97 to the Bulletin of the EU

Slovakia

Page 21, left column, first line after the title "Economic structure":

"6.3 %" should be replaced by **"5.6 %"**.

Page 24, left column, second and third line after the title "Foreign trade":

"57 %" should be replaced by "**63 %**", and "1996" by "**1995**".

On pages 21, 85 and 87 the tables should be replaced by the following tables
(corrected figures are shown in negative).

Page 21:

Main indicators of economic structure

(all data for 1996 unless otherwise indicated)

Population	*million*	5.4
GDP per head	*PPS-ECU (1995)*	7 100.0
as % of EU-15 average	*% (1995)*	41.0
Share of agriculture in:		
value-added	*% (1995)*	5.6
employment	*% (1995)*	9.7
Gross foreign debt/GDP	*%*	43.0
Exports of goods and services/GDP	*% (1995)*	63.0
Stock of foreign direct investment[1]	*billion ECU*	0.6
	ECU per head	110.0

[1] FDI stock converted at end 1996 exchange rate of ECU 1 = USD 1.25299.
Source: Commission services, national sources, EBRD

1.3. General evaluation ... 19

2. Economic criteria ... 20

2.1. The economic situation ... 20

Background ... 20

Liberalization ... 22

Stabilization of the economy ... 22

Structural change ... 24

Financial sector ... 25

Economic and social development ... 26

2.2. The economy in the perspective of membership ... 27

Introduction ... 27

The existence of a functioning market economy ... 27

The capacity to cope with competitive pressure and market forces ... 28

Prospects and priorities ... 30

2.3. General evaluation ... 30

3. Ability to assume the obligations of membership ... 31

3.1. Internal market without frontiers ... 31

The four freedoms ... 31

— General framework ... 32

— Free movement of goods ... 33

— Free movement of capital ... 35

— Free movement of services ... 36

— Free movement of persons ... 38

— General evaluation ... 39

Competition ... 40

3.2. Innovation ... 41

Information society ... 41

Education, training and youth ... 42

Research and technological development ... 42

Telecommunications ... 43

Audio-visual ... 44

3.3. Economic and fiscal affairs   45

Economic and monetary union   45

Taxation   46

Statistics   48

3.4. Sectoral policies   49

Industry   49

Agriculture   51

Fisheries   55

Energy   55

Transport   57

Small and medium enterprises   58

3.5. Economic and social cohesion   59

Employment and social affairs   59

Regional policy and cohesion   60

3.6. Quality of life and environment   61

Environment   61

Consumer protection   63

3.7. Justice and home affairs   64

3.8. External policies   65

Trade and international economic relations   65

Development   66

Customs   67

Common foreign and security policy   68

3.9. Financial questions   68

Financial control   68

Budgetary implications   69

4. Administrative capacity to apply the *acquis*   70

4.1. Administrative structures   70

4.2. Administrative and judicial capacity   71

4.3. General evaluation   74

C. Summary and conclusion   75

Annex   79

Composition of Parliament   81

Single market: White Paper measures   82

Statistical data   84

A. Introduction

a) Preface

The application for membership

Slovakia presented its application for membership of the European Union on 27 June 1995, and the Council of Ministers decided on 17 July 1995 to implement the procedure laid down in Article O of the Treaty, which provides for consultation of the Commission.

That is the framework in which the Commission submits the present opinion, responding to the request of the European Council in Madrid in December 1995 to present the opinion as soon as possible after the conclusion of the Intergovernmental Conference, which commenced in March 1996 and concluded in June 1997.

The context of the opinion

The Slovak application for membership is being examined at the same time as applications from nine other associated countries. Slovakia's accession is to be seen as part of an historic process, in which the countries of Central and Eastern Europe overcome the division of the continent which has lasted for more than 40 years, and join the area of peace, stability and prosperity created by the Union.

The European Council in Copenhagen in June 1993 concluded that:

'The associated countries in Central and Eastern Europe that so desire shall become members of the Union. Accession will take place as soon as a country is able to assume the obligations of membership by satisfying the economic and political conditions. Membership requires:

☐ that the candidate country has achieved stability of institutions guaranteeing democracy, the rule of law, human rights and respect for and protection of minorities;

☐ the existence of a functioning market economy, as well as the capacity to cope with competitive pressure and market forces within the Union;

☐ the ability to take on the obligations of membership, including adherence to the aims of political, economic and monetary union.

The Union's capacity to absorb new members, while maintaining the momentum of European integration, is also an important consideration in the general interest of both the Union and the candidate countries.'

This declaration spelled out the political and economic criteria for examining the accession requests of the associated countries of Central and Eastern Europe.

The European Council in Madrid in December 1995 referred to the need, in the context of the pre-accession strategy, 'to create the conditions for the gradual, harmonious integration of the applicant countries, particularly through:

☐ the development of the market economy,

☐ the adjustment of their administrative structure,

☐ the creation of a stable economic and monetary environment'.

In its opinion, the Commission analyses the Slovak application on its merits, but also according to the same criteria as the other applications, on which it is delivering opinions at the same time. This way of proceeding respects the wish, expressed by the European Council in Madrid, to ensure that the applicant countries are treated on an equal basis.

In addition to the individual opinions, the Commission is presenting separately to the Council, in the framework of its communication 'Agenda 2000', a general assessment of the accession requests, and its recommendations concerning the strategy for successful enlargement of the Union. At the same time, it is presenting an evaluation of the impact of enlargement on the Union's policies.

The contents of the opinion

The structure of the opinion takes account of the conclusions of the European Council in Copenhagen. It:

☐ describes the relations up to now between Slovakia and the Union, particularly in the framework of the association agreement;

☐ analyses the situation in respect of the political conditions mentioned by the European Council (democracy, rule of law, human rights, protection of minorities);

□ assesses Slovakia's situation and prospects in respect of the economic conditions mentioned by the European Council (market economy, capacity to cope with competitive pressure);

□ addresses the question of Slovakia's capacity to adopt the obligations of membership, that is the *acquis* of the Union as expressed in the Treaty, the secondary legislation, and the policies of the Union;

□ makes, finally, a general evaluation of Slovakia's situation and prospects in respect of the conditions for membership of the Union, and a recommendation concerning accession negotiations.

In assessing Slovakia in respect of the economic criteria and its capacity to assume the *acquis*, the Commission has included a prospective assessment; it has attempted to evaluate the progress which can reasonably be expected on the part of Slovakia in the coming years, before accession, taking account of the fact that the *acquis* itself will continue to develop. For this purpose, and without prejudging the actual date of accession, the opinion is based on a medium-term time horizon of approximately five years.

During the preparation of the opinion, the Commission has obtained a wealth of information on Slovakia's situation from the Slovak authorities, and has utilized many other sources of information, including the Member States and numerous international organizations.

b) Relations between the European Union and Slovakia

Historical and geopolitical context

Slovakia is a mountainous, landlocked country situated centrally in Europe and sharing borders with Austria, the Czech Republic, Poland, Hungary and Ukraine. It has an area of 49 000 km² and a population of 5.3 million.

Slavs have inhabited the Slovak lands since the fifth century. From the 10th to 20th centuries, the Slovak lands were part of the Hungarian and Austro-Hungarian Empire, apart from a period of partial Turkish occupation after 1526. In the 19th century a sense of Slovak national identity emerged, partly in reaction to policies of Magyarization applied to the Slovak lands.

The Czechoslovak Republic was proclaimed in October 1918. Its composition was multi-ethnic: 51% Czech, 23% German, 14% Slovak and 5.5% Hungarian, according to a 1921 census. The country inherited 60-70% of the industrial base of the Austro-Hungarian Empire.

In the 1930s the Sudeten Germans' demands for autonomy created increasing tension. Under the 1938 Munich Agreement and the Vienna Arbitration the regions bordering Germany and mostly settled by Germans were ceded to Germany, and a quarter of the Slovak lands ceded to Hungary. In March 1939 German troops occupied the rest of the Czech lands and Slovakia became a nominally independent State under President F. Jozef Tiso.

After the war the Czechoslovak Republic was restored to its pre-war borders, except for Ruthenia, which was annexed by the Soviet Union. Virtually all Sudeten Germans were forced to leave Czechoslovak territory and their possessions were confiscated.

Czechoslovakia was one of the founding members of the post-war international economic institutions (IMF and IBRD in 1945, GATT in 1948). But after the formation in 1948 of a government composed of only Communists and their allies the Communist Party expanded its hold on power. Under the division of labour agreed within Comecon Czechoslovakia concentrated on developing its heavy industry. In the 1960s central controls were partially relaxed. Reform pressures within the Communist Party resulted in the election of Alexander Dubcek as First Secretary in January 1968. The introduction of democratic elements into political and cultural life, known as the Prague Spring, was brought to a brutal end by invasion by members of the Warsaw Pact on 21 August 1968, which led to re-imposition of Soviet orthodoxy under Gustav Husak.

Nevertheless, a small dissident movement, later associated with the Charter 77 group, remained active through the 1970s and 1980s. The political unrest in many countries of Central and Eastern Europe in 1989 led to protests in Czechoslovakia in November of that year. Popular reaction to the violent police repression of a student demonstration in Prague on 17 November led to Husak's abdication and the election the following month of Vaclav Havel, a leading member of Charter 77, as President.

After 1989, the name of the country was officially changed to the Czech and Slovak Federal Republic. Differences between Czech and Slovak politicians on the future federal structure and economic policy became unbridgeably wide. In October 1992 the parliaments of the two republics passed a joint resolution dissolving the federation and creating two independent successor States as of 1 January 1993.

The political situation during the first year of independence was unstable: though there was consensus on the need for political and economic reform, there were sharp differences over the pace and nature of the latter. Between March and September 1994 a multi-party interim government replaced the first post-independence government. Elections in September 1994 led to the formation of a coalition government, whose term-in-office has been characterized by turbulence between it and the other institutions of the State.

Slovakia's position concerning the European Union

The Czechoslovak Government, which was formed in 1990, committed itself clearly to European integration. This commitment was reflected in the signature of the Europe Agreement in March 1992. The Slovak Government assumed the positive policy stance towards Europe integration as well as the rights and obligations under the Europe Agreement concluded by the federation. The policy of the current Slovak Government towards the European Union was set out in its programme of January 1995. This stated that its foreign policy priorities included membership of Slovakia in the EU; and underlined its commitment to implement fully the Europe Agreement, to approximate legislation and standards to those of the EU, to prepare for entry into EMU and to proceed with full trade liberalization. The memorandum accompanying the Slovak application for membership submitted on 27 June 1995 states 'The strategic objective of the Slovak Republic is to become a ful-fledged member in the EU within the time horizon around the year 2000. The Slovak Republic wishes to join the EU as an equal member actively contributing to the advantageous multi-faceted cooperation'.

Contractual relations

Diplomatic relations between the European Community and the Czechoslovak Republic were established in September 1988. The first agreement between them was the four-year Trade Agreement on Industrial Products which entered into force in April 1989. A Trade and Cooperation Agreement was concluded in 1990. In the autumn of 1990 the Union proposed to Czechoslovakia, and to Hungary and Poland, conclusion of Association Agreements, to be known as Europe Agreements to support their political and economic transformation. The agreement with Czechoslovakia was signed on 16 December 1991. Its trade provisions entered into force in March 1992 by way of an Interim Agreement replacing the 1989 agreement. The Interim Agreement provided for the consolidation of previous trade concessions as well as the gradual and asymmetric establishment of a free trade area over a period of 10 years. The division of Czechoslovakia made it necessary to negotiate new Europe Agreements with the two successor states. The agreement with Slovakia was signed in October 1993 and entered into force in February 1995.

The Europe Agreement is the legal basis for relations between Slovakia and the Union. Its aim is to provide a framework for political dialogue, promote the expansion of trade and economic relations between the parties, provide a basis for Community technical and financial assistance, and an appropriate framework to support Slovakia's gradual integration into the Union. The institutional framework of the agreement provides a mechanism for implementation, management and monitoring of all areas of relations. Subcommittees examine questions at a technical level. The Association Committee, at senior official level, provides for discussion of, and often solutions to, problems arising under the agreement. The Association Council, at ministerial level, examines the overall status of, and perspectives for, relations and provides the opportunity to review Slovakia's progress on preparation for accession.

The Slovak Government has established a coordinated institutional framework for dealing with European integration matters and specifically for the implementation of the Europe Agreement. At ministerial level, there is a Council for Integration into the European Union, chaired by the Deputy Prime Minister. His deputies are the Minister for Foreign Affairs and the Deputy Prime Minister responsible for approximation of legislation. Each Slovak ministry has a department responsible for all EU related matters and is represented in this Council depending on the European integration issues being discussed. In 1996 a parliamentary committee on European integration was established.

The pre-accession strategy

Implementation of the Europe Agreement and the White Paper

The institutional framework of the Europe Agreement is fully functional. The Association Council has met three times; the Association Committee twice. The Joint Parliamentary Association Committee has also met on four occasions. A structure comprising nine multidisciplinary subcommittees has been established to assist the Association Committee. The full range of issues has been discussed. The political circumstances in Slovakia have made necessary a particular focus on issues relating to the establishment of civil society.

The trade provisions have been implemented according to schedule, but there have been some delays regarding the entry into force of some of the other provisions of the agreement. The implementing rules on competition entered into force on 1 January 1997 instead of March 1995 as foreseen under the agreement. Those on State aids are only now being finally approved. Slovakia has not yet implemented its commitments on intellectual and industrial property.

Most of the trade problems which have arisen in the implementation of the Europe Agreement have been successfully resolved. The use of balance of payments restriction measures has figured importantly amongst those problems. The Slovak Government maintained an import surcharge in place from 1994 to 1 January 1997, longer than necessary in light of balance of payments developments. The government introduced an import deposit scheme in May 1997 on balance of payments grounds, which is still under discussion. Technical barriers to trade have arisen because of differences in the Slovak standards and certification rules. Slovakia notified the EU in mid-1996 of its intention to start discussion with Russia of a possible free trade agreement. After discussion within the instances of the agreement, Slovakia modified its intentions to seeking no more than trade liberalization in certain areas.

The Commission's White Paper of 1995 on the internal market set out the legislation which candidate countries would have to transpose and implement in order to apply the *acquis*, and identified elements essential to the implementation of the single market (known as Stage I measures) which would need priority attention. Slovakia has attached considerable importance to the legal tasks related to transposition. The Slovak Government has published a strategy for implementing the White Paper. This fits into an overall strategy for legislative approximation which sets out priorities which should result in the entry into effect of EC internal market legislation in the medium term. Progress in legislative alignment has been achieved in the area of banking, free movement of capital, indirect taxation, agriculture and environment.

With the exception of the intellectual property area, the Slovak Government has consistently met its obligations under the Europe Agreement and has shown a willingness to cooperate in the resolution of the problems which have arisen. Its attachment to balance-of-payment restrictions is, however, evidence of some continuing unease at its obligations under the agreement.

Structured dialogue

Slovakia has participated in the structured dialogue and has submitted background documents for a number of the structured dialogue meetings. At the joint ministerial meeting (foreign affairs) on 29 October 1996 the Slovak Government submitted a paper on the status of implementation of the preaccession strategy in Slovakia, which included suggestions for improving the structured dialogue, by focusing on accession-related agenda items and involving the associated countries more in choosing them.

Phare

From 1990 to 1996, ECU 212 million have been allocated to the Slovak Republic under the Phare programme, ECU 4 million thereof being allocated to cross-border cooperation in 1995. In 1996, Slovakia received only a commitment for ECU 4.5 million. Main sectors of activity had previously been the development of the private sector, infrastructure development, human resources development and European integration, including support to public administration reform and approximation of legislation.

The Phare programme has had programming and implementation problems. In 1996, no funds were committed to either national or cross-border programmes, because of administrative bottlenecks and Slovakia's low absorption rate, but also because Slovakia rejected a funding proposal due to its conditionality. The situation has since improved.

Participation in Community programmes

Slovakia has adopted the Additional Protocol to the Europe Agreement on Community programmes and is ready to participate initially in Socrates, Leonardo and Youth for Europe as from 1997. As from 1998, participation will be extended to include MEDIA II, Kaleidoscope, Raphael, Ariane and health and social programmes as well.

Trade relations

Between 1989 and 1992 trade between the EU and Czechoslovakia increased dramatically. EU imports jumped from ECU 2.6 billion to ECU 5.5 billion (+ 112%) and EC exports from ECU 2.4 billion to ECU 6.3 billion (+ 163%). With the dissolution of Czechoslovakia, the Czech Republic became Slovakia's largest trading partner, receiving 42% of Slovak exports in 1993 and 37% in 1994. But more than half of the 23.5% jump in Slovak exports from 1993 to 1994 resulted from increased exports to the EU. Between 1993 and 1995 EU (12) imports from Slovakia increased from ECU 1.15 billion to ECU 2.61 billion (+ 124%). For the first half of 1996, EU (15) imports were ECU 1 688 million. EU (12) exports to Slovakia increased from ECU 1.2 billion in 1994 to ECU 2.69 billion (+ 126%) in 1995. For the first half of 1996, EU (15) exports were ECU 1 884 million. Apart from 1994 when the EU was in deficit of ECU 80 Million with Slovakia, the overall balance of trade has remained in surplus for the European Union. The EU is now the fastest growing and the biggest trade partner. Germany alone takes up about half of EU trade with Slovakia.

Slovakia remains largely specialized in a limited number of product lines, especially chemicals, iron and steel products, textiles and apparel. Slovakia's most important imports from the Union are machinery and electrical articles, transport equipment and chemical products. The most important Slovak exports to the EU were base metal and articles, textiles, transport equipment and machinery and electrical articles.

Slovakia has a customs union with the Czech Republic and is a founding member of the Central Europe Free Trade Agreement (CEFTA). The Czech Republic is Slovakia's single most important trading partner, absorbing 31% of Slovak exports and providing 24.5% of Slovak imports in 1996. Poland, Hungary, Romania and Bulgaria are also important export markets.

General evaluation

The EU-Slovak relationship has developed under the Europe Agreement. Trade-related issues have been relatively few, although the import deposit scheme remains to be resolved. A wide range of other issues have also had to be addressed within the relationship: political issues; disagreement over management of the PHARE programme; and the future of Slovakia's nuclear power programme. The Slovaks have been willing to use the machinery of the relationship to address such issues, even though not all of them have been resolved.

B. Criteria for membership

1. Political criteria

The European Council in Copenhagen decided on a number of 'political' criteria for accession to be met by the candidate countries in Central and Eastern Europe. These countries must have achieved 'stability of institutions guaranteeing democracy, the rule of law, human rights and respect for and protection of minorities'.

In carrying out the assessment required in this connection, the European Commission has drawn on a number of sources of information: answers given by the Slovak authorities to the questionnaire sent to them by Commission staff in April 1996, bilateral follow-up meetings, reports from Member States' embassies and the Commission's delegation, assessments by international organizations (including the Council of Europe and the OSCE), reports produced by non-governmental organizations, etc.

The following assessment involves a systematic examination of the main ways in which the public authorities are organized and operate, and the steps they have taken to protect fundamental rights. It does not confine itself to a formal description but seeks to assess the extent to which democracy and the rule of law actually operate.

This assessment relates to the situation in June 1997. It does not examine in detail any changes which have taken place in the past or which may come about in the future, though it generally takes account of any stated intention to reform a particular sector. The situation of the government is mentioned here only in passing: it will be examined in greater depth in Chapter 4.

1.1. Democracy and the rule of law

The Constitution adopted in September 1992, at the same time as the declaration of independence and national sovereignty, established Slovakia as a parliamentary democracy. However, the operation of institutions in Slovakia has encountered a number of difficulties.

Parliament and legislative powers: structure

The parliament is unicameral – the National Council of the Republic of Slovakia – and comprises 150 members elected for four years by proportional representation. Only parties which have received at least 5% of the votes cast (7% in the case of a coalition of two or three parties, 10% if the coalition has four or more parties) are allocated seats in parliament.

The large number of political groupings (there are 79 registered parties) testify that there is a genuine multi-party system in Slovakia. Parties which received over 3% of the votes in the last election are entitled to State financing.

The President of the Republic may dissolve the National Council if the government has been defeated on a vote of confidence three times in the six months following parliamentary elections. At any other time, a parliamentary vote with a two-thirds majority is the only means of securing a dissolution.

Article 78 of the Constitution guarantees members of parliament the traditional immunities.

Parliament exercises legislative power and shares its right of initiative with the government. The government and the individual ministers can make regulations within the limits laid down by law.

The President of the Republic may organize referendums, at the request either of parliament or of at least 300 000 citizens. Referendums are required to confirm constitutional laws or decide that Slovakia should accede to, or withdraw from, a union of States. They may cover any subject other than basic rights, the tax system or the national budget.

Functioning of parliament

Elections in Slovakia are free and fair. The latest parliamentary elections, in September 1994, brought into power a coalition government led by the 'Movement for a democratic Slovakia', which had lost its majority in March of that year following internal disputes (see annex for results of the last parliamentary election).

Parliament in Slovakia does not carry out its duties in conditions which comply with the normal rules for the operation of democracy.

The rights of the opposition are not fully respected, particularly with regard to its membership of parliamentary committees. From September 1994 to January 1997 there was no provision for the opposition to have a proportional share of the seats on the parliamentary committees of enquiry responsible for monitoring the secret services and the armed forces' intelligence services. These committees have not yet been established because the government has refused to accept the members appointed by the opposition to sit on them. In addition, the opposition chairs none of parliament's standing committees, although it did so up to September 1994.

Respect for the mandates of members of parliament and the procedures governing the work of parliament is not always guaranteed. The resignation as a member of parliament of Mr Gaulieder, which he contests, is currently being examined by the Constitutional Court. Since 1994 the parliamentary majority has also established four committees of enquiry composed almost exclusively of its own members. Of these committees, two are responsible for investigating the circumstances surrounding the overthrow of the government in March 1994, one is concerned with the secret services and the other deals with the armed forces' intelligence services. The Constitutional Court has criticized the establishment of these committees because their terms of reference exceed the powers granted to parliament by the Constitution.

The executive: structure

The President of the Republic is elected by a three-fifths majority of parliament for a five-year term, renewable once only. He exercises the traditional prerogatives of a head of State. He may be dismissed by parliament by a three-fifths qualified majority if he acts contrary to the sovereignty or territorial integrity of the country or its constitutional and democratic system. He may ask the National Council to reconsider a law which it has adopted, but the Council may override his veto by a simple majority.

The Slovak Constitution contains the risk of an institutional impasse if a majority cannot be found for the appointment of a new President of the Republic. If this post is vacant, it appears that a new government cannot be appointed and the incumbent Prime Minister assumes the prerogatives of the President.

The President appoints the Prime Minister and, on his proposal, the ministers. Both the government and the individual ministers are responsible to parliament.

Administratively, the country is divided into eight regions and 79 districts headed by government representatives. The law of July 1996 increased the powers of these bodies at the expense of those hitherto exercised by local authorities. However, the allocation of responsibilities between the decentralized levels of the national government and the local authorities still remains to be clarified.

Slovakia has only one type of local authority, the municipality, of which there are 2 680. They are financed both from their own resources and from a share of national tax revenue determined each year by the national government.

The Slovak administration has no civil service code clearly defining the rights and obligations of civil servants. This makes it more difficult to combat the problems of corruption which the country is experiencing.

The army and police are under the control of the civil authorities while the secret services are responsible directly to the Prime Minister. In theory, their activities are subject to parliamentary scrutiny.

Functioning of the executive

The main weakness of the way the executive power operates in Slovakia is that the present government does not fully respect the role and responsibilities of the other institutions and frequently adopts an attitude which goes beyond the confrontations traditionally accepted in a democracy.

The constant tension between the government and the President of the Republic is an example of this situation. In 1995 the majority party began proceedings to dismiss the President although the conditions required for this (see above) were clearly not satisfied. This process failed because the government was unable to get the two-thirds majority required by the Constitution. In 1996 the operating budget for the Presidency was sharply reduced.

Similarly, in October 1995 civil servants were invited to sign a petition from the Minister for Culture seeking the dismissal of the President. Those who did not wish to sign were threatened with sanctions. Such inter-institutional conflict goes well beyond what is normally acceptable in democratic politics.

In a démarche on 25 October 1995, the European Union expressed its concern about the political and institutional tension prevailing in Slovakia and in particular about measures being taken against the President of the Republic which could infringe the Constitution and run counter to normal democratic practice in the Union. In a resolution adopted in November that year, the European Parliament took a similar line.

When referendums were organized on 23 and 24 May 1997 on the accession of Slovakia to NATO and the election of the President of the Republic by direct universal suffrage, the government – following the ruling of the Constitutional Court that the referendum on the method of electing the President was compatible with the Constitution – refused to distribute voting papers to polling stations bearing this question and defied the decision of the central referendum committee, which accordingly ruled that the voting on 23 and 24 May had not proceeded in accordance with the law.

The government also sought to extend its methods of exercising control over various sectors of civil society. The process of privatization was carried out in conditions which did not meet the requirements of transparency and fairness. The mechanisms for carrying it out were criticized by the Constitutional Court. The law on higher education adopted in 1996 gives the government greater powers to intervene in the appointment of university teachers.

There is inadequate control of the work of the secret services in Slovakia by the civil authorities, particularly parliament. Such control is exercised only by the government, which has not yet allowed the introduction of parliamentary control which the opposition fully supports. The relevant authorities have not completed the investigations required into certain matters in which the involvement of these services was suspected such as the kidnapping of the son of the President of the Republic, the killing of the agent Remias and the attack on the editor-in-chief, head of 'Sme', Peter Toth.

The judiciary: structure

The independence of the judicial system in Slovakia is impeded in a number of respects. Judges are appointed by parliament acting on a proposal from the government, initially for a four-year term and then for an unlimited period. This 'probationary period' provided for in Article 145 of the Constitution may restrict the independence of judges, particularly during their early years in office. The Minister for Justice also has the power, which he has already used, to transfer the presidents and vice-presidents of judicial districts at his discretion. On the other hand, judges can be dismissed only by parliament after it has received the opinion of a disciplinary board and only for serious reasons. They enjoy the same immunities as members of parliament, which can be removed only by the

Constitutional Court. Judges, like prosecutors, may not be members of political parties.

The prosecutor's office, under the authority of a prosecutor-general appointed and removed by the President, acting on a proposal from parliament, is independent of the executive. However, the bill establishing the organization of the prosecutor's office and the status of its members provided for in Article 151 of the Constitution has not yet been passed into law.

The civil courts are responsible for the control of administrative acts.

Slovakia has no ombudsman.

The Constitutional Court, established in 1993, comprises 10 members appointed for a seven-year term by the President of the Republic from a list of 20 names put forward by parliament. It monitors the conformity of laws and regulations with the Constitution and international treaties. It settles conflicts which may arise between the various constitutional powers, judges parliamentary elections and referendums and may rule on appeals against the dissolution of a political party or the removal from office of a member of parliament.

Under Article 130 of the Constitution, a decision by the government or the administration may be referred to the Constitutional Court by one fifth of the members of parliament, the President of the Republic, the government, the prosecutor-general, the courts or any person who considers that his basic rights or liberty has been infringed and who has been unable to secure redress from other courts.

Functioning of the judiciary

The judicial process in Slovakia is marked by excessive delays, and judges would benefit from stronger guarantees of their independence.

The Constitutional Court has played a very active role in endeavouring to keep a balance between the various powers and preserving their respective responsibilities as defined by the Constitution. Since 1994 the Court has ruled 12 bills to be unconstitutional.

1.2. Human rights and the protection of minorities

Slovakia has set in place a number of norms to ensure observance of human rights and the rights of minorities. Various international conventions are also applicable, above all the European Convention on Human Rights and its main additional protocols. In accordance with Article F of the TEU, this collection of texts forms part of the *acquis*; any country wishing to join the Union must have ratified them.

Slovakia, which has been a member of the Council of Europe since June 1993, has been a party to the European Convention on Human Rights and its additional protocols since March 1992 as a result of the ratifications carried out by Czechoslovakia. It has also granted private individuals the right to appeal to the European Court of Human Rights if they consider that their rights under that convention have been violated.

Among other international conventions protecting human rights and minorities, Slovakia has ratified the convention against the use of torture and the framework convention on minorities. It has also ratified the main UN conventions on human rights.

Under the Slovak Constitution, international conventions on human rights take precedence over national law if they are more favourable.

Civil and political rights

Access to the judicial system is largely guaranteed in Slovakia. Legal aid is available in criminal cases.

The death penalty was abolished in 1990 and is forbidden under the Constitution in all circumstances.

There is protection against arbitrary arrest. Nobody may be arrested without a warrant issued by a public prosecutor and must be brought before a judge within 24 hours. During that period, an accused person has the right to a lawyer. Within 24 hours of the arrest, a judge must decide whether the person should be released or charged. Remand may not exceed a period of one year unless the Supreme Court decides to extend this period because of the special risk to society presented by the detained person.

All citizens over 18 years of age have guaranteed electoral rights.

Freedom of association is guaranteed in Slovakia, as is demonstrated by the expanding number of associations (12 000 NGOs in the country). Parliament has adopted a law on foundations imposing stricter conditions which will prevent some previously registered NGOs from conforming to the requirements in the future. Parliament is currently considering a bill on non-profit-making organizations.

The right of assembly is guaranteed in Slovakia.

The government has exercised considerable influence on the public radio and television networks, marked in particular by a very substantial imbalance in the amount of access granted to the government and the opposition. A growing private audio-visual sector (a private national television network, five local networks, and 20 private radio stations) has substantially increased freedom of expression. This trend is being supported by the growing number of foreign radio and television stations (49 cable broadcasting licences).

There is substantial variety in the press (11 national daily newspapers and seven which cover more than one region) although the government-inclined *Slovenska Republika* receives substantial public finance.

After the President had twice referred back the draft amendment to the criminal code containing severe restrictions on freedom of expression and the freedom of assembly which the European Union had criticized strongly in April 1996, parliament finally rejected the bill.

The right to property is recognized and expropriation may take place only in the public interest and with fair compensation. Slovakia has established an efficient system to restore property to those who were deprived of it during the communist regime. It has restored the property of various religious communities.

Respect for privacy is assured as the police require a warrant before undertaking any search or telephone tapping.

Slovakia has ratified the Geneva Convention on Refugees, and asylum-seekers enjoy the internationally guaranteed rights and protection.

A number of cases of the police inflicting inhuman and degrading treatment on persons in preventive detention have been reported recently.

Economic, social and cultural rights

The Slovak Constitution recognizes the right to the minimum income required for survival, and to social security.

Trade union freedoms (except for members of the armed services) are guaranteed by Article 37 of the Constitution. There are currently four trade union federations in Slovakia and the 'Trade Union Confederation' (KOZ) is by far the largest. Almost 80% of workers are members of a trade union.

The right to strike is recognized by Article 37(4) of the Constitution for all except judges, prosecutors, the armed forces and firemen. Although there have been few strikes in Slovakia since 1989, this right is exercized regularly and encounters no particular obstacles.

Freedom of education and religion are guaranteed by the Constitution. Fifteen denominations and religious organizations are recognized and receive financial assistance from the State. However, it should be noted that broadcasts on the public television networks have recently explained that the Jews were deported from Slovakia because they 'enriched themselves at the expense of the Slovak people'. The Slovak authorities recently published a school textbook idealizing the pro-Nazi Slovak regime. The government withdrew the book on 1 July 1997.

Minority rights and the protection of minorities

Minorities in Slovakia make up between 18% and 23% of the population, principally Hungarians (11%) and gypsies or Roma (4.8% to 10% depending on estimates).

Minorities are protected first of all by a number of international norms. In September 1995 Slovakia ratified the Council of Europe's framework convention on minorities. However, it has not subscribed to Recommendation 1201 of the Parliamentary Assembly of the Council of Europe which provides for the collective rights of minorities, although is not legally binding. Following the signature in March 1995 of a treaty of friendship and cooperation with Hungary, the Slovak Parliament accompanied ratification in March 1996 by two declarations denying recognition of collective rights for minorities and removing the possibility of establishing ethnically based autonomous administrative structures.

The Constitution grants minorities the right to develop their own culture, to receive information and education in their own language and to participate in taking decisions which concern them. The State budget includes funding to encourage cultural and educational activities for minorities. There are no specific provisions guaranteeing the representation of minorities in parliament but since the September 1994 elections the Hungarian minority has had 17 members of parliament belonging to three parties in a coalition. Slovakia has also complied with the recommendations of the Council of Europe on names (Hungarians are no longer obliged to translate their surnames into Slovak) and the use of the minority language alongside Slovak on road signs where minorities account for more than 20% of the population.

While the minorities live harmoniously alongside the rest of the population of Slovakia, there are nevertheless some tensions between the government and the Hungarian minority.

The first problem arises from the law on the national language of November 1995, which repealed the earlier provisions allowing the use of a minority language for official communications in any town or village where the minority represented more than 20% of the population. The Slovak authorities had given commitments to the European Union and the OSCE's High Commissioner for national minorities that it would adopt a new law on the use of minority languages. It should also be noted that Article 34(2) of the Slovak Constitution expressly states that minorities may use their own language for official communications and that the arrangements for exercising that right should be laid down by law.

Nevertheless, Slovakia has not yet passed comprehensive legislation on this point and has gone back on the commitments it gave earlier. It is true that other texts govern the use of minority languages in specific fields (public life, courts, radio and television, public schools and road signs) but these do not cover all situations and there is still no overall text.

This ambiguous situation is further aggravated by certain government decisions concerning the Hungarian minority, such as reductions in the subsidies granted to Hungarian cultural associations and the cessation of bilingual school reports in Hungarian schools (a teacher not respecting this rule can be dismissed).

The gypsies or Roma, whose numbers grew in Slovakia after partition, continue to suffer considerable discrimination in daily life and are quite frequently the target of violence from skinheads against which they receive only inadequate protection from the police. Their social position is often difficult, although here sociological factors play a part, alongside the discrimination they suffer from the rest of the population, particularly with regard to access to employment, housing and public services in general (unemployment of about 40 to 50%).

1.3. General evaluation

The position of Slovakia raises a number of problems from the point of view of the conditions set by the Copenhagen European Council.

Two of the main features of the way institutions in Slovakia operate are that the government pays insufficient respect to the powers devolved by the Constitution to other bodies and too frequently disregards the rights of the opposition. The constant tension between the government and the President of the Republic is one example of this situation. Similarly, the way in which the government recently ignored decisions by the Constitutional Court and the central referendum committee on the voting which took place on 23 and 24 May 1997 directly threatens the stability of the institutions. The frequent refusal to involve the opposition in the operation of the institutions, particularly where parliamentary scrutiny is concerned, underlines this trend.

Against this background, the use made by the government of the police and the secret services gives cause for concern and substantial efforts will have to be made to provide better guarantees of the independence of the judicial system and of satis-factory conditions for its operation. The fight against corruption also needs to be made more effective.

Improvement is also required in the treatment of the Hungarian minority, which still does not benefit from the general law on the use of minority languages which the Slovak authorities have undertaken to introduce and for which there is provision in the Constitution. The position of the Roma (gypsies) also requires attention from the authorities.

In view of the points set out above, while the institutional framework defined by the Slovak Constitution corresponds to that of a parliamentary democracy with free and fair elections, the situation with regard to the stability of the institutions and their integration into political life is unsatisfactory. Despite recommendations made by the European Union on the occasion of a number of approaches and statements, there has been no appreciable improvement.

2. Economic criteria

In examining the economic situation and prospects of Slovakia, the Commission's approach is guided in particular by the conclusions of the European Council in Copenhagen in June 1993, which stated that membership of the Union requires 'the existence of a functioning market economy, as well as the capacity to cope with competitive pressure and market forces within the Union'.

This section of the opinion therefore gives a concise survey of the economic situation and background, followed by a review of Slovakia's progress in key areas of economic transformation (liberalization of the price and trade system, stabilization of the economy, structural change, reform of the financial sector) as well as its economic and social development. It concludes with a general evaluation of Slovakia in relation to the criteria mentioned by the European Council and a review of prospects and priorities for further reform.

2.1. The economic situation

Background

Slovakia, with a population of 5.4 million, had a gross domestic product (GDP) of ECU 38 billion (expressed in purchasing power parity) in 1995; its population is about 1.5% of that of the Union, while its economy is only about 0.6% and GDP per head is about 41% of the Union average. However, at ECU 220 the average monthly wage is low by western standards.

Slovakia is a founding member of the WTO and CEFTA, and its application for membership to the OECD is currently under review.

Progress in economic transformation

Before World War II, Czechoslovakia was one of the richer countries in Europe, but the Slovak part of the country remained mainly rural and was much poorer. Under the communist regime, Czechoslovakia espoused central planning in its entirety, and started to invest heavily in the industrialization of Slovakia, based on cheap imports of raw materials and energy from the Soviet Union. By 1989, after almost half a century of central planning, Czechoslovakia's economy had dropped far behind even the poorest Member States, but economic activity was more evenly spread over the country.

The fall of the communist regime in November 1989 led to the creation of the democratic Czech and Slovak Federal Republic (CSFR). The situation at the beginning of transition was relatively favourable for the CSFR: excess demand was not really present, fiscal and monetary policies had been prudent for a number of years, and the external debt was small. The 'monetary overhang' (unwanted savings caused by shortages) was limited, so inflation did not soar as much as in other countries in the region. The reform process was started immediately: prices and trade were liberalized, privatization proceeded rapidly, economic institutions were established, and new bankruptcy and competition legislation was introduced. However, due to the structure of its industry, Slovakia was hit harder by the loss of eastern markets, and opposition to reforms grew. The failure to reach an agreement on the future course of economic policy was an important element in the decision to split the CSFR.

Since late 1992, Slovakia has had to face the difficult tasks of building a market economy and, at the same time, establishing the institutions of an independent State. The process of separation from the Czech Republic compounded the economic difficulties. Political instability and the lack of a broad social consensus on the path of economic reform presented additional obstacles to the transformation process. Also, the termination of transfers from the Czech Republic unmasked large underlying fiscal and external imbalances. On the positive side, Slovakia inherited a very low external debt, low inflation and a tradition of orthodox and sound macroeconomic policy.

A programme of rapid privatization began in 1991, and by the time of the separation of the CSFR, small-scale privatization and the first wave of large-scale privatization were virtually completed. After independence, preparations for a second wave of

voucher privatization were started, but after a change of government, this second wave was cancelled and replaced by direct sales in June 1995.

Foreign direct investment

Foreign direct investment remains very low (only 0.8% of GDP in 1996; source: EBRD), despite there being few legal barriers. The main reasons for this seem to be the lack of foreign confidence in the commitment of the authorities towards market reform, the exclusion of foreigners in most of the privatization process, and political uncertainty.

Economic structure

Agriculture accounts for about 6.3% of value added, and employs 9.7% of the working population. After the start of transition, and in particular price liberalization, the collapse of agricultural production was sharper than the reduction of overall production. However, agricultural production also recovered faster and started to grow again already in 1993.

Before 1989, over 80% of cultivated land was owned by collective or State farms. Since then, legislation has been introduced to return the land to the original owners, to transform the collective farms into privately owned cooperatives, and to privatize the State farms. Nevertheless, in practice the structure of the agricultural sector has not yet been changed drastically. Only few State farms have actually been privatized, because of uncertainty over land restitution claims, the lower quality of their land, outdated machinery, and high debts. Although the members of cooperatives can redraw their part

Main indicators of economic structure

(all data for 1996 unless otherwise indicated)

Population	*million*	5.4
GDP per head	*PPS-ECU (1995)*	7 100.0
as % of EU-15 average	*% (1995)*	41.0
Share of agriculture in:		
value-added	*% (1995)*	5.6
employment	*% (1995)*	9.7
Gross foreign debt/GDP	*%*	43.0
Exports of goods and services/GDP	*% (1995)*	57.0
Stock of foreign direct investment[1]	*billion ECU*	0.6
	ECU per head	110.0

[1] FDI stock converted at end 1996 exchange rate of ECU 1 = USD 1.25299.
Source: Commission services, national sources, EBRD

of the land and assets to set up a new individual farm, the cooperatives still own the major part of the land. Most individual farms remain small and produce mainly for own consumption.

Industry accounts for about one third of GDP, and a somewhat higher share in employment. The communist regime invested mainly in the development of heavy industry in Slovakia. Important parts of the sector have been privatized, and about 70% of industrial production is now produced in private enterprises. The steel and petrochemical sectors, which are both dominated by one big enterprise, are now competitive and able to export to western markets. However, the growth potential in these sectors remains limited given the existing excess capacity across Europe. Likewise, the chemicals and non-ferrous metal sectors are technically advanced and internationally competitive. Other sectors, such as textiles and the important defence industry, face a considerable restructuring effort to ensure survival.

Important parts of the services sector (major banks, telecommunications) are still controlled by the State. Tourism is a potential growth sector for Slovakia, but will need considerable investment as it has been neglected under the communist regime.

Liberalization

Price regime

In 1991, 85% of consumer prices were liberalized. By 1995 some 10% were still administered, mainly for energy, some public services and rents. In 1996, a price law was adopted that gives far-reaching powers to the administration to assess the justification of large price changes. Although so far this legislation has only been used to control prices of a limited number of agricultural products, it could also be applied to control normal market or seasonal fluctuations, which would distort the role of market price signals.

Trade regime

In general, Slovakia has a liberal and transparent trade regime, characterized by moderate tariffs and by the infrequent use of non-tariff barriers. After the dissolution of the CSFR, the two new republics formed a 'customs union', with a common external tariff, but without free circulation of goods coming from third countries. Slovakia has reached trade agreements with the EU, EFTA and CEFTA, and is a founding member of the WTO.

In 1993, a 10% import surcharge was introduced as a temporary measure to support the precarious balance-of-payments situation. Although the external account improved considerably in 1994 and 1995, the surcharge was maintained. Under pressure from the EU and the WTO, the government lowered the surcharge rate to 7.5% on 1 July 1996, and to 0% on 1 January 1997.

In May 1997, the Slovak Government introduced an import deposit scheme. Under this measure, importers will have to make a non-interest-bearing deposit of 20% of the value of imports in a Slovak bank for six months. This deposit scheme was introduced as a reaction to a similar measure introduced by the Czech Government in April 1997, and with the intention to improve the rapidly worsening current account balance. Although the cost increasing effect of the measure is limited, the measure can effectively block all imports by small importers that do not have sufficient access to the financial markets to finance the deposit. Consequently, the exact effect of the measure on the trade deficit is hard to predict. Nevertheless it is clear that this move is an unfortunate step backwards.

Foreign exchange regime

Slovakia's strengthened external position made it possible to introduce full current account convertibility of the Slovak crown on 1 October 1995. This operation, which was originally planned for 1 January 1996, was brought forward because the Czech Republic ended the Czech-Slovak clearing system for bilateral trade payments on that date.

The exchange rate is fixed to a basket of the German mark (60%) and the US dollar (40%), with a fluctuation margin that has gradually increased from ± 1.5% in 1995 to ± 7% now. It can be expected that the National Bank of Slovakia (NBS) will increasingly use the wider exchange rate margins as an additional instrument to fulfil its monetar policy objectives.

Stabilization of the economy

Domestic

The loss of the traditional export markets resulting from the break-up of the CMEA, aggravated by the disrupted trade with the Czech Republic after the dissolution of the federation, put Slovakia in a deep recession from 1989 to 1993, during which period GDP fell by almost one quarter. 1994 saw a sharp recovery, initiated by rising exports to the EU and the Czech Republic. The leading role of exports was gradually taken over by domestic demand, resulting in some of the highest GDP growth rates in the region during 1995 and 1996. Economic growth is now completely driven by domestic demand and the economy risks overheating. If macroeconomic policies remain restrictive, this should not result in re-emerging inflationary pressures in the short term. Nevertheless, the external balance has already been affected by the sizeable growth of domestic demand. The longer-term development of the Slovak economy will not only depend on continued sound macroeconomic policies, but also on micro-economic factors, such as the degree of restructuring of banks and enterprises. Indeed, non-inflationary high growth can only be maintained when competitiveness increases sufficiently.

As a result of tight monetary and fiscal policies, inflation remained limited during the transition period. Only in 1991, as a result of the price liberalization, and in 1993, because of the introduction of VAT, were higher inflation rates recorded. Since then, inflation steadily declined to reach 5.8% on average in 1996, the lowest rate of the associated transition countries. However, because of the buoyancy of domestic demand and some adjustment of administered prices, inflation accelerated again in the first months of 1997. Therefore, it is expected that the inflation rate will not continue its downward trend in 1997.

In sharp contrast to the evolution in the Czech Republic, unemployment rose very quickly in Slovakia after the start of transition. Unemployment peaked twice at 15.2%, in January 1994 and in January 1995, but declined to 12.8% at the end of 1996. However, in the first quarter of 1997, unem-ployment was higher than in the corresponding period of 1996. It remains unevenly spread over the country, and the proportion of long-term unemployed is high. Only a small part of the high economic growth is translated into additional employment because of the high growth rate of labour productivity.

During the first year of independence, the general government deficit rose to 7.6% of GDP as a consequence of the termination of fiscal transfers from the Czech Republic, and of difficulties of setting up a new tax administration. Public finances improved considerably in 1994 and were approximately in equilibrium in 1995, mainly resulting from higher-than-expected tax receipts, generated by higher growth. The stance of fiscal policy has become more expansionary in 1996, with an estimated general government deficit of 1.3% of GDP. In the State budget for 1997, expenditures are further increased compared to the outcome of 1996, resulting in a higher planned deficit for 1997. However, an important proportion of the increased expenditures will be used for necessary investment in infrastructure.

External

Slovakia inherited a low foreign debt from the CSFR, and debt remained relatively low after independence. Thanks to its stability-oriented economic policy, Slovakia has gained access to private capital markets and has obtained investment-grade ratings from the major credit rating agencies.

Main economic trends

		1994	1995	1996
Real GDP growth rate	%	4.9	6.8	6.9
Inflation rate				
annual average	%	13.3	9.9	5.8
December on December	%	11.6	7.2	5.4
Unemployment rate, endyear	%	13.3	12.8	10.9
	(ILO definition)			
General government budget balance	*% of GDP*	– 1.3	0.1	– 1.3
Current account balance	*% of GDP*	4.8	2.3	– 10.2
Debt/export ratio	%	47.9	53.1	71.6
Foreign direct investment inflow	*% of GDP*	1.3	1.0	0.8

Source: Commission services, national sources, EBRD

As a consequence of the dissolution of the federation, Slovak exports to the Czech Republic were reduced by one third in 1993. Nevertheless, because of the repressed domestic demand, and after a devaluation of the koruna and the introduction of a 10% import surcharge – a temporary additional tax on imports – the current-account balance recovered quickly from a deficit of more than 5% of GDP in 1993 to a surplus of almost 5% in 1994. However, in 1996 the continued growth of domestic demand pushed up imports of consumer and investment goods considerably, while exports stagnated, resulting in a rapid deterioration of the current account to a deficit of more than 10% of GDP.

The evolution of the foreign exchange reserves clearly shows the overall improvement of the balance of payments. Reserve holdings of the National Bank almost doubled in 1995, and represented four months of imports of goods and services, compared with only 2.4 months at the end of 1994. However, with the deterioration of the current account, the reserve position has deteriorated significantly in recent months. Without a significant increase of foreign direct investment, the reserve position might be threatened in the longer term, if the high current account deficit is maintained.

Structural change

Foreign trade

The Slovak Republic has a very open economy with exports of goods and services accounting for 57% of GDP in 1996.

External trade has been substantially reoriented towards western markets, and in particular to the Union. The EU is now the fastest growing and the biggest trade partner, accounting for around 36% of Slovak imports and 41% of exports. Germany alone takes up almost half of the EU trade with Slovakia. Despite its diminishing share, the Czech Republic remains the most important single country for trade with Slovakia, representing about one quarter of imports and almost one third of exports. One fifth of imports still come from the former Soviet Union (FSU), mainly energy and raw materials, but the FSU accounts for less than one tenth of all exports.

The most important import product categories are machinery and equipment, energy, intermediate goods, and chemicals. As a consequence of higher investment, imports of machinery and equipment are growing fastest. In 1996, 38.3% of exports consisted of intermediate goods (mainly steel), 23.2% of machinery and transport equipment, and 12.4% of chemicals. Exports of steel, cars, and chemicals are each time dominated by only one enterprise.

Labour market

After the start of the transition process, unemployment in Slovakia increased much faster than in the Czech Republic, although the macroeconomic and structural policy frameworks were the same under the CSFR. This can be explained by Slovakia's higher dependence on exports to CMEA markets, its important defence industry, and the higher reliance on cheap imports of energy and raw materials from the former Soviet Union, which all led to a sharper reduction of employment. Furthermore, the Slovak labour force did not decline as much as in the Czech Republic because retirement was lower than in the Czech Republic.

Unemployment stabilized when the economy recovered in 1994, and started to decline in 1995. This positive evolution is mainly the result of additional employment creation. The decline of the participation rate is now largely completed, after the initial exit of women and older workers from the labour market. More than half of the unemployed have been out of work for more than a year. Long-term unemployment is particularly widespread among people with a low education level. Given the continued potential for high labour productivity growth, it can be expected that future unemployment reductions will only be gradual.

Real wages began growing again in 1994. More recently, real wage growth has even exceeded productivity gains, which risks harming competitiveness.

Public finances

The initial public finance conditions after independence were particularly difficult in Slovakia: the costs of establishing a new State and a new administration were aggravated by the continuing economic recession, the ending of the important fiscal transfers from the federation, and the difficulties associated with the reform of the tax system (introduction of VAT). As a result, the initial objective of a balanced budget for 1993 proved to be unrealistic, and a general government deficit of 7.6% was recorded.

Because of tight expenditure control and higher-than-expected tax receipts, generated by higher economic growth and improved tax collection, public finances recovered considerably in 1994 and 1995, when a small general government surplus was recorded. As a result of higher expenditures, mainly infrastructure investment, and a lowering of the VAT rate, the deficit rose again in 1996, and is planned to be almost 2% of GDP in 1997. In the future, there is a risk that the restructuring of the banking sector could have negative effects on the budget, because of a possible introduction of tax deductibility for provisions on bad loans, or because of the calling in of State guarantees on bad debt. However, according to the government's programme, the general government deficit should be kept below 3% of GDP.

The structure of government finances has changed considerably. On the expenditure side, subsidies to enterprises were reduced and the social security system was moved from the State budget to separate institutions, which are financed by social security contributions. Social security expenditures are relatively high (about one third of general government expenditures), especially for pensions. On the revenue side, the turnover tax was replaced by a value-added tax, and personal income and corporate profit taxes were introduced. Revenues from personal income tax remain low compared to other sources of revenue.

Enterprise sector: privatization and enterprise restructuring

A first wave of voucher privatization was concluded under the CSFR. To avoid excessive dispersion of ownership, the Slovak authorities decided to cancel the second wave of voucher privatization and replace it by direct sales. Most enterprises were sold to the management and workers at preferential prices, with the possibility of extending payments over a period of up to 10 years. In general, the second wave of privatization has lacked transparency and was considered as inequitable.

Progress on enterprise restructuring has not been fully satisfactory in Slovakia. Besides a core group of highly profitable enterprises, there is still a relatively large group of loss makers, which need to restructure to survive. The main reasons for the lack of enterprise restructuring are the continued involvement of the State, a weak banking sector, ineffective bankruptcy procedures, and insufficient foreign direct investment. Consequently, the enterprises do not have to face a sufficiently 'hard budget constraint' – there is still an expectation by enterprise managers that the government or the banks will bail them out when they incur losses.

The authorities are trying to maintain their influence on important decisions in privatized enterprises that are considered strategic. Although the constitutional court has removed the legal basis for the compulsory creation of 'golden shares', which would have given the government a veto on important decisions, the government is trying to convince the new owners of privatized enterprises to obtain the same result on a voluntary basis. Moreover, the proposed law on the revitalization of enterprises would increase the government's influence on strategic enterprises in difficulty. The draft law foresees possibilities to reschedule or cancel debts to the budget and banks, through a secretive and untransparent procedure, with an important political involvement.

Slovakia has not been able to attract significant amounts of foreign direct investment, while the scale of the bad debt problem prevents domestic banks from playing an active role in financing enterprise restructuring. Most new owners of privatized enterprises will typically also lack the financial means for investment, since they already had to invest to acquire the control of the company. Consequently, investment for restructuring will mainly have to be financed out of retained earnings of the enterprises, which is only possible for already profitable entities. Only the biggest of these profitable enterprises might also be able to finance their restructuring efforts on the international capital markets.

Little progress has been made in the implementation of an effective bankruptcy law. The current 1993 law includes conciliation procedures and exemptions that obstruct a quick and just procedure. Furthermore, the courts are overburdened and inexperienced. The proposed law on the revitalization of enterprises would add an additional hurdle for creditors to file bankruptcy proceedings, because the enterprises that would be selected for restructuring under the provisions of this law would be exempt from bankruptcy for the period of the revitalization programme.

Financial sector

The authority responsible for monetary policy is the National Bank of Slovakia, which was created on 1 January 1993, taking over from its federal predecessor. It is independent from the government, and is responsible for monetary and exchange rate policy, as well as banking regulation and supervision. Interest rates have been fully liberalized and, following the abolition of the remaining credit ceilings on individual banks in

January 1996, monetary policy is now fully exerted through indirect instruments. Banking regulation and supervision have been progressively strengthened.

The number of banks operating in Slovakia has increased from only 4 at the end of 1991 to 29: 10 without foreign capital participation, 14 with foreign capital participation, and 5 branches of foreign banks. There are also 10 representative offices of foreign banks. Participations by the State, foreign capital and private domestic capital take up about equal shares of the subscribed capital of banks. However, the banking system remains heavily concentrated in the three largest banks, which are still mainly State owned. The shares of the three biggest banks in total loans and deposits are about 65 and 70% respectively. Privatization of these banks is currently under discussion. It has recently been decided that two of the major banks (VUB and IRB) can be privatized, but that the Savings Bank, which still holds most of the private deposits, and the State Insurance Company, the largest insurer in Slovakia, will remain in State hands until 2003. It is not yet clear which method will be used for the privatization of VUB and IRB, and if foreign participation in the privatization process will be invited.

Despite direct assistance from the State and the banks' own work-out efforts, the proportion of non-performing loans remains relatively high: loans reported as overdue by at least three months represented almost one third of outstanding loans at the end of 1995. The large majority of these bad loans is held by State-controlled banks, and most debtors are State-owned enterprises, which often benefit from State guarantees. The authorities favour a gradual solution of the bad-debt problem by imposing further provisioning by the banks. The State intends to support this process, but no decision has yet been taken on the form, size and conditions of the State participation in bank restructuring. While 73% of the risk of the bad loans is now covered by provisions and reserves, their weight remains excessive and puts a significant burden on the profitability of the banking sector. Consequently, to support their financial position, the banks have to maintain relatively high margins between deposit and lending rates, which limits the possibilities of the banking sector to support enterprise restructuring by providing credits at acceptable rates.

The main tendency in enterprise and personal sector lending is a continuous decrease in the personal lending share and a growing share of enterprise lending in the total amounts of bank lending. Credits in foreign currency also grew considerably in recent years, although their share in the total lending remained relatively low (around 10%). In 1995 there was an increase in the share of private borrowers in the total volume of banks loans. In that year short-term loans accounted for 75% of the total volume of new loans drawn by private organizations. Share issues do not represent an alternative financing source for companies, while bond issues are more widely used as source of corporate finance. The market for short-term funds is not yet fully developed, although it has the structure and features of money markets in mature market economies.

Capital markets remain fragmented and illiquid, and the legislative framework needs to be further developed. The first wave of voucher privatization gave an impulse to the trade in shares, with an important intermediary role for the investment privatization funds (IPFS). However, the unexpected cancellation of the second wave of voucher privatization in 1995, and the more restrictive regulation on IPFS, reduced market confidence considerably, and limited further market development. Trade in privatization bonds, which were issued as a compensation for the cancelled vouchers, has remained marginal due to a lack of demand and a legally imposed minimum price.

Economic and social development

Social indicators

Slovakia has an estimated population of 5.4 million. Population growth has been declining almost continuously from 1.8% a year in the mid-1950s to less than 0.5% now. This slowing of population growth implies a gradual ageing of the population, and a rising share of the population of working age. Life expectancy at birth in 1996 was 68.4 years for men and 76.3 years for women.

The education level is relatively high. Secondary education has been concentrated on vocational and technical specializations, which reflects the importance of heavy industries and engineering in the economy.

Regional and sectoral differences

Regional differences are particularly pronounced in Slovakia, certainly when the relatively small size of the country is taken into account. Production is mainly concentrated in the western part of the country (Bratislava and neighbouring districts) and around Kosice, in eastern Slovakia. As a result, unemployment is also very unevenly spread, varying from 4% in Bratislava to more than 20% in the more rural districts. A reduction of regional differences in unemployment levels is obstructed by relatively underdeveloped transport and communication infrastructure in rural regions, and low geographical labour mobility, partly as a result of scarce and expensive housing in regions with the fastest economic growth.

2.2. The economy in the perspective of membership

Introduction

The European Council in Copenhagen in 1993 defined the conditions that the associated countries in Central and Eastern Europe need to satisfy for accession. The economic criteria are:

☐ the existence of a functioning market economy;

☐ the capacity to cope with competitive pressure and market forces within the Union.

These criteria are linked. Firstly, a functioning market economy will be better able to cope with competitive pressure. Secondly, in the context of membership of the Union, the functioning market is the internal market. Without integration into the internal market, EU membership would lose its economic meaning, both for Slovakia and for its partners.

The adoption of the *acquis*, and in particular the internal market *acquis*, is therefore essential for a candidate country, which must commit itself permanently to the economic obligations of membership. This irreversible commitment is needed to provide the certainty that every part of the enlarged EU market will continue to operate by common rules.

The capacity to take on the *acquis* has several dimensions. On the one hand, Slovakia needs to be capable of taking on the economic obligations of membership, in such a way that the single market functions smoothly and fairly. On the other hand, Slovakia's capacity to benefit fully from the competitive pressures of the internal market requires that the underlying economic environment be favourable, and that the Slovak economy have flexibility and a sufficient level of human and physical capital, especially infrastructure. In their

absence, competitive pressures are likely to be considered too intense by some sections of society, and there will be a call for protective measures, which, if implemented, would undermine the single market.

The capacity and determination of a candidate country to adopt and implement the *acquis* will be crucial, since the costs and benefits of doing so may be unevenly spread across time, industries and social groups. The existence of a broad based consensus about the nature of the changes to economic policy which membership of the Union requires, and a sustained record of implementation of economic reforms in the face of interest group pressure reduce the risk that a country will be unable to maintain its commitment to the economic obligations of membership.

At the level of the public authorities, membership of the Union requires the administrative and legal capacity to transpose and implement the wide range of technical legislation needed to remove obstacles to freedom of movement within the Union and so ensure the working of the single market. These aspects are examined in later chapters. At the level of individual firms, the impact on their competitiveness of adopting the *acquis* depends on their capacity to adapt to the new economic environment.

The existence of a functioning market economy

The existence of a market economy requires that equilibrium between supply and demand be established by the free interplay of market forces. A market economy is functioning when the legal system, including the regulation of property rights, is in place and can be enforced. The performance of a market economy is facilitated and improved by macroeconomic stability and a degree of consensus about the essentials of economic policy. A well-developed financial sector and an absence of significant barriers to market entry and exit help to improve the efficiency with which an economy works. Good progress in the implementation of the Europe Agreement should also help to consolidate the functioning of the market economy.

Slovakia has implemented most of the necessary reforms to establish a market economy. The price system has been liberalized, allocation decisions are decentralized by the almost completed privatization process, and an independent judicial system is in place, which has proved on several occasions that it is able to protect property rights. In general, there are no significant legal barriers to market entry. The economy has also attained a satisfactory sustainable level of macroeconomic stability, including the lowest inflation rate of the region, which allows economic agents to have a sufficiently long-planning horizon.

Nevertheless, on a number of occasions, the Slovak authorities have been favouring non-market-based mechanisms for price formation or resource allocation. Examples of this are the very low proportion of competitive sales of State enterprises in the privatization process, the setting of a minimum price on the sale of privatization bonds, and the efforts of the government to maintain control on enterprises that are considered strategic. These are clear indications that the functioning of the market economy still needs to be reinforced.

A limited number of prices – mainly energy, some public services and rents – are still administered, which distorts relative prices. The regulation of prices of public services can be considered to be in line with existing practices in Member States. However, the continued subsidies on household energy consumption have negative effects on energy efficiency and the trade balance. The curbs on rents increase the concentration of economic activity in certain regions, and reduces private investment in residential construction. Moreover, the more restrictive Price Law of 1996 could be used to apply controls on normal or seasonal price fluctuations, thus distorting the role of market price signals.

A strong and stable financial sector is an essential element of a functioning market economy. The Slovak financial sector still has considerable restructuring problems to resolve, such as the high proportion of non-performing loans and the dominance of a limited number of State-owned banks. Consequently the sector is not yet able to play its intermediation role to the full extent. Moreover, capital markets remain illiquid and fragmented, and progress is still needed in their regulation. Nevertheless, while these problems reduce the efficiency with which the economy functions, the financial system is sufficiently developed not to hinder the normal functioning of the economy.

In a number of important sectors (steel, banking, petrochemicals) there is little domestic competition, with the bulk of production often concentrated in one enterprise. Market dominance of a limited number of enterprises can be an impediment for the entrance of new enterprises in these sectors.

Nevertheless, the trade regime is sufficiently open to foreign competition to guarantee competitive behaviour on the domestic market.

Little progress has been made in the implementation of an effective bankruptcy law. The current legislation includes conciliation procedures and exemptions that obstruct a quick and just procedure. Furthermore, the courts are overburdened and inexperienced. The proposed Enterprise Revitalization Act would add an additional hurdle for creditors to file bankruptcy proceedings, because the enterprises that would be selected for restructuring under the provisions of this law would be exempt from bankruptcy for the period of the revitalization programme.

The capacity to cope with competitive pressure and market forces

It is difficult, some years ahead of prospective membership, and before Slovakia has adopted and implemented the larger part of Community law, to form a definitive judgment of the country's ability to fulfil this criterion. Nevertheless, it is possible to identify a number of features of Slovakia's development which provide some indication of its probable capacity to cope with competitive pressure and market forces within the Union.

This requires a stable macroeconomic framework within which individual economic agents can make decisions in a climate of a reasonable degree of predictability. There must be a sufficient amount of human and physical capital including infrastructure to provide the background, so that individual firms have the ability to adapt to face increased competitive pressures in the single market. Firms need to invest to improve their efficiency, so that they can both compete at home and take advantage of economies of scale which flow from access to the single market. This capacity to adapt will be greater, the more firms have access to investment finance, the better the quality of their workforce, and the more successful they are at innovation.

Moreover, an economy will be better able to take on the obligations of membership the higher the degree of economic integration it achieves with the Union ahead of accession. The more integrated a country already is with the Union, the less the further restructuring implied by membership. The level of economic integration is related to both the range and volume of goods traded with Member States. Direct benefits from access to the single market may also be greater in sectors where there are a sizeable proportion of small firms, since these are relatively more affected by impediments to trade.

The Slovak economy has a number of important assets to be able to face competitive pressure and market forces in the single market. The economy is stabilized and rapidly growing, while wage costs remain relatively low, and the population is well-educated. The central location on the crossing of important north-south and west-east trans-European network (TEN) corridors could also contribute to the development of a competitive services sector, if sufficient investment in these corridors takes place.

Slovakia has also been able to re-orient its exports towards west European markets, after the loss of its traditional export markets resulting from the break-up of the CMEA and the dissolution of the federation with the Czech Republic. The high growth rates of trade with the Union in recent years are not only an indication that at least a number of Slovak enterprises are sufficiently competitive to export to the EU, but also that they are able to produce goods that comply with the rules and regulations of the single market.

Another indicator of competitiveness is the capacity of enterprises to adjust. Although the traditionally important heavy industrial enterprises in the steel and petrochemical sectors are now capable of supplying quality basic products, at competitive prices, the growth potential in these sectors remains limited given the existing excess capacity in Europe. Likewise, the chemicals and non-ferrous metal sectors are technically advanced and internationally competitive. Other sectors, such as textiles and the important defence industry, face a considerable restructuring effort to ensure survival. In general, additional investment will be needed in all sectors to modernize and restructure production capacity, and to adapt it to fulfil the requirements of the *acquis*. Efforts will have to be made to diversify towards lighter assembly industries and services, which are more in line with Slovakia's natural endowments. However, the present capacity of Slovakia to innovate and diversify production is hampered by limited expenditure on research and development. Imports of skills and technology from abroad also remain limited because of insufficient foreign direct investment.

The diversification and restructuring effort could be hampered by a lack of investment capital. So far, Slovakia has not been able to attract significant amounts of foreign direct investment, while the financing capacity of the domestic financial sector remains limited by the bad-debt problem. Most new owners of privatized enterprises will typically also lack the financial means for investment, since they already had to invest to acquire the control of the company. Consequently, investment for restructuring will mainly have to be financed out of retained earnings of the enterprises, which is only possible for already profitable entities. Only the biggest of these profitable enterprises might also be able to finance their restructuring efforts on the international capital markets. Therefore, a restructuring, probably associated with some form of re-capitalization, of the financial sector, is an essential pre-condition to support enterprise restructuring in general, but in particular of small and medium-sized enterprises, which do not have easy access to international capital markets. Given the constraints on the government budget, such a revitalization of the financial sector is probably only possible in combination with its privatization. Foreign involvement in the privatization process seems to be essential, in order to introduce the necessary skills and capital into the sector.

Slovakia could, in principle, resolve its remaining economic problems sufficiently rapidly to be among the first associated countries to join the Union. However, the uncertainty remains as to whether these structural problems will be tackled swiftly, and whether it will be done in a transparent way, using market mechanisms that are compatible with the rules of the single market. The reason for this doubt is the fact that economic policy in recent years has been characterized by a lack of predictability and transparency. The most prominent examples of this can be found in the privatization process, where the second voucher programme was unexpectedly cancelled, the role of IPFS was changed abruptly (causing important losses for these funds), and the privatization of the major banks has been announced and postponed again several times. The proposed law on enterprise revitalization also lacks transparency because the choice of enterprises that benefit from this legislation is subject to political influence. Moreover, the Slovak authorities are still relying frequently on non-market-based mechanisms for price formation or resource allocation.

A sufficiently convincing track record of consistent economic reform is still missing. The announcement and implementation by the Slovak authorities of a comprehensive, transparent and market-oriented medium-term structural reform programme would help to attract the necessary support of foreign investors, and would enable the Slovak economy to be sufficiently competitive to face the competition in the single market at the time of accession.

Prospects and priorities

The economic policies of the Slovak Republic have not yet been guided by an elaborated medium-term programme. Documents exist on some aspects of economic policy (monetary policy, industrial policy, etc.), but they are mainly short term and not integrated in one general blueprint. Nevertheless, in the framework of the association subcommittee on economic issues, the Slovak authorities have declared their willingness to elaborate a comprehensive medium-term stabilization and modernization strategy. This would help to determine future reform priorities, in order to tackle the remaining economic difficulties.

In its first years of independence, Slovakia has achieved remarkable progress in macroeconomic stabilization. Of all associated Central European countries, it recorded in 1995 and 1996 among the highest GDP growth rates, combined with the lowest inflation rate of the region. However, while the current account remained positive in 1995, continued high domestic demand for consumption and investment goods has turned it sharply into deficit in 1996. Some acceleration of inflation in the first quarter of 1997, and the high current account deficit, are clear indications that the economy is now starting to overheat. In order to guarantee the continued stability of the economy, macroeconomic policies need to be sufficiently restrictive, and need to be well coordinated. Additionally, microeconomic factors, such as the degree of restructuring of banks and enterprises, will also have to be improved. Indeed, non-inflationary high growth can only be maintained when the competitiveness of the economy increases sufficiently.

Once the difficulties of establishing a new State and a new administration were overcome, the general government budget deficit was rapidly reduced, and even recorded a small surplus in 1995. However, the stance of fiscal policy became more expansionary in 1996, as a result of lower than expected revenues and the need for higher public investment. Because of budgetary costs associated with restructuring the enterprise and banking sectors, government deficits are expected to rise in the coming years. The upward pressure on expenditures could be alleviated by targeting social expenditures to those who really need them. Also, completion of price liberalization would allow further reduction of subsidies to enterprises.

Although unemployment has been declining in recent years, the high unemployment rate and its considerable regional variation will continue to put a burden on future economic and budgetary developments. Although the unemployment problem cannot be solved overnight, support for creating new small and medium-scale enterprises, a more flexible labour market, limiting the fiscal burden on wage costs by tightening access to social security programmes, and higher regional wage differences to promote inter-regional mobility, could all accelerate employment creation.

To ensure sustained economic growth, Slovakia will need continued enterprise and financial sector restructuring. Given the choice for a gradual approach to the solution of the bad-debt problem, the banking sector will not be able to be a major source of financing for enterprise restructuring in the short term. Further restructuring will have to be financed from abroad, or from internally generated enterprise resources. Foreign direct investment has so far remained limited because of a lack of confidence in the market-orientation of policy-makers. Moreover, restructuring will probably not be helped by the continued efforts of the government to maintain influence in already privatized enterprises, and by the untransparent procedures of the proposed Enterprise Revitalization Act.

2.3. General evaluation

Slovakia has introduced most of the reforms necessary to establish a market economy. The price system has been liberalized, and allocation decisions are decentralized by the advanced privatization process. Nevertheless, a restrictive price law was introduced in 1996, and the draft Enterprise Revitalization Act would be a major step back from market mechanisms. The financial sector needs to be reinforced, and progress is needed in the regulation of the bankruptcy process and capital markets.

Slovakia should be able to cope with competitive pressure and market forces within the Union in the medium term, but this would require more transparent and market-based policies. For a number of years, the economy has grown rapidly, with low inflation. The country has low wage costs and a skilled labour force. However, enterprise restructuring has been slow, which is gradually undermining economic growth and external balance. The low level of foreign direct investment reflects these structural problems, which need to be tackled swiftly and in a transparent way.

3. Ability to assume the obligations of membership

The European Council in Copenhagen included among the criteria for accession 'the ability to take on the obligations of membership, including adherence to the aims of political, economic and monetary union'.

In applying for membership on the basis of the Treaty, Slovakia has accepted without reserve the basic aims of the Union, including its policies and instruments. This chapter examines Slovakia's capacity to assume the obligations of membership – that is, the legal and institutional framework, known as the *acquis*, by means of which the Union puts into effect its objectives.

With the development of the Union, the *acquis* has become progressively more onerous, and presents a greater challenge for future accessions than was the case in the past. The ability of Slovakia to implement the *acquis* will be central to its capacity to function successfully within the Union.

The following sections examine, for each main field of the Union's activity, the current and prospective situation of Slovakia. The starting-point of the description and analysis is a brief summary of the *acquis*, with a mention of the provisions of the Europe Agreement and the White Paper, where they are relevant. Finally, for each field of activity there is a brief assessment of Slovakia's ability to assume the obligations of membership on a medium-term horizon.

3.1. Internal market without frontiers

Article 7(a) of the Treaty defines the Union's internal market as an area without internal frontiers in which the free movement of goods, persons, services and capital is ensured. This internal market, central to the integration process, is based on an open-market economy in which competition and economic and social cohesion must play a full part.

Effective implementation of the liberties enshrined in the Treaty requires not only compliance with such important principles as, for example, non-discrimination or mutual recognition of national regulations – as clarified by Court of Justice rulings – but also concomitant, effective application of a series of common specific provisions. These are designed, in particular, to provide safety, public health, environmental and consumer protection, public confidence in the services sector, appropriately qualified persons to practise certain specialist occupations

and, where necessary, introduction or coordination of regulatory and monitoring mechanisms; all systematic checks and inspections necessary to ensure correct application of the rules are carried out on the market, not at frontier crossings.

It is important to incorporate Community legislation into national legislation effectively, but even more important to implement it properly in the field, via the appropriate administrative and judicial structures set up in the Member States and respected by companies. This is an essential pre-condition for creating the mutual trust indispensable for smooth operation of the internal market.

This chapter must be read in conjunction with, *inter alia*, the chapters on social policy, the environment, consumer protection and sectoral policies.

The four freedoms

A step-by-step approach is being taken to absorption of the *acquis* by the applicant countries:

☐ The Association Agreement between the Community, its Member States and Slovakia came into effect on 1 February 1995. With regard to the four freedoms and approximation of legislation, the agreement provides, in particular, for immediate or gradual application of a number of obligations, some of them reciprocal, covering, in particular, freedom of establishment, national treatment, free trade, intellectual property and public procurement.

☐ The Commission's 1995 White Paper (COM(95) 163 final) guidelines, intended to help the applicant countries prepare for integration into the internal market, gives a closer definition of the legislation concerned. It identifies the 'key measures' with a direct effect on the free movement of goods, services, capital and persons and outlines the conditions necessary in order to operate the legislation, including the legal and organizational structures. Twenty-three areas of Community activity are examined, dividing the measures into two stages, in order of priority, to provide a work programme for the pre-accession phase. The Technical Assistance and Information Exchange Office (TAIEX) was set up with the objective of providing complementary and focused technical assistance in the areas of legislation covered in the White Paper. A legislative database has recently been established by the office.

☐ The applicant countries will have to transpose and implement all the *acquis*. The 'action plan for the single market' submitted to the Amsterdam European Council gives details of the priority measures necessary to make the single market work better among the 15 current Member States in preparation for introduction of the single currency. This will inevitably entail changes to the *acquis*.

General framework

Whatever their field of activity, undertakings must be able to operate on the basis of common rules. These are important since they shape the general framework within which economies operate and, hence, the general conditions of competition. They include the rules on competition (on undertakings and State aid) and tax measures discussed elsewhere in this opinion, the opening-up of public works, supply and service contracts, harmonization of the rules on intellectual property (including the European patent), harmonization of the rules on company law and accountancy, protection of personal data, transfer of proceedings and recognition of judgments (Article 220 EC Conventions).

Descriptive summary

Public procurement is regulated by the Act on procurement of goods, services and public works passed in 1993 which has since been amended. The Ministry of Building and Public Works is in charge of managing the various aspects of public procurement policy.

With regard to intellectual and industrial property, Slovakia is a member of TRIPs (trade related aspects of intellectual property rights) and undertook to apply its provisions since 1 January 1996. An Industrial Property Office has been set up. The responsibility for intellectual property issues rests with the Ministry of Culture.

Company law is governed by a number of different statutes, in particular the Commercial Code. A variety of kinds of enterprise exists in the Slovak Republic, including public trading companies, limited liability companies and joint stock companies. As of 31 March 1997, there were 2 957 joint stock companies and 34 495 limited liability companies registered. Only joint stock companies are entitled to issue shares to raise finance and shareholders appear to be protected in this event. Minimum capital requirements are laid down by law. Creditors appear to be afforded a basic level of protection. A commercial register is kept with the key elements of information about trading companies, which is open to anyone on payment of a

modest fee. Such companies are obliged to disclose details of changes relating to them. Details of non-trading companies are kept with the Ministry of Interior or the district office of state administration.

With regard to accounting, the Act on Accountancy (1991) provides the basic framework for the annual accounts of companies. A Regulation from the Ministry of Finance (1993) provides for the drawing up of consolidated accounts. It is not clear how accounting standards are set. According to the Act on Auditors (1992), the Chamber of Auditors regulates the position and activities of auditors.

The protection of fundamental rights of physical persons is enshrined in the Slovak Constitution and in Act 256/1992 on the protection of personal data.

Current and prospective assessment

The Slovak legislation on public procurement contains some of the fundamental principles of the EC public procurement rules. However, it lacks clarity and detail, not fully meeting all the requirements of the EC Directives. This is particularly true as regards the utilities sectors (energy, telecommunications, water and transport). In addition, it remains to be seen whether the review procedures in place are rapid and effective enough. The legislation in force does not provide any preferential treatment to Slovak suppliers and therefore exceeds Europe Agreement obligations in this respect. The government plans to amend the existing law on public procurement in the course of 1997 with a view to achieving full compatibility with the EC Directives.

Concerning intellectual and industrial property, Slovakia has not yet ensured a level of protection similar to that existing in the EC, as provided for in Article 67 of the Europe Agreement. An application for accession to the Munich Convention on the granting of patents was submitted in early 1997.

Although trade mark legislation adopted on 1 March 1997 is, according to the Slovak authorities, in full conformity with EC legislation, only partial approximation has been achieved in regard to patents and semi-conductors legislation. Copyright legislation in conformity with EC legislation is expected to be adopted in the course of 1997. Full conformity in all legislation in the intellectual and industrial property area is envisaged by the Slovak authorities by 2000.

Effective implementation and enforcement will remain a significant concern in the medium term due to the lack of experience of the authorities involved and to the current weakness of internal control and border enforcement mechanisms.

On the basis of the information on company law provided by the Slovak Republic, the law relating to trading companies already appears to be in conformity with the first and second Directives. As for the law on other companies, and the third, eleventh and twelfth Directives, it is understood that all legislation currently in force is being examined and full harmonization is intended to be achieved by 2000.

Amendments to the Act on Accountancy and the Act on Auditors are foreseen for the first quarter of 1998. Amendments to the regulation on consolidated accounts are foreseen during the second half of 2000. These changes are intended to bring about full conformity with the fourth, seventh and eighth Directives, but draft texts are not yet available. Certain transitional problems are in evidence relating to the implementation in practice of the new rules, including a shortage of qualified accountants and auditors, and major efforts will be required if these are to be solved in the medium term.

The current legislation in the data protection field does not comply with the EC framework Directive. Legislative changes are needed in particular to enable the creation of an independent authority to supervise the application of legislation. A draft law which aims at compatibility with the Directive has been drawn up and the Slovak authorities expect that legislation will be adopted and implemented in the medium term. Slovakia has not yet acceded to the Council of Europe Convention No. 108 on data protection.

On the subject of civil law, Slovakia has not yet been invited to accede to the Convention of Lugano on matters of competent jurisdiction and the execution of civil and commercial decisions. The States already party to the convention must first assess whether there has been progress in the protection of civil interests.

Conclusion

Slovakia is progressively adopting important measures in compliance with the provisions of the Europe Agreement and the White Paper's recommendations especially in regard to company law, public procurement and intellectual and industrial property. However, in all of these areas, new legislation and legislative amendments to complete the alignment process are needed.

In the public procurement and intellectual and industrial property areas, a major effort has to be made to strengthen the implementation and enforcement structures so as to ensure the effective application of the legislation.

The information so far available on accounting and auditing does not provide a sufficient basis on which to make a detailed assessment of its present conformity with the *acquis*, or Slovakia's prospects of achieving it, although the timetable for reform seems reasonable. Slovakia already has several years of experience in implementing data protection legislation, but improvements still need to be made in the legislation and implementing structures.

Free movement of goods

Free movement of goods can be achieved only by removing measures which restrict trade – not only customs duties and quantitative restrictions but all measures with equivalent, namely protectionist, effect, irrespective of whether or not they are specifically aimed at domestic or imported products. Where technical standards are not harmonized, the free movement of goods must be ensured by applying the principle of mutual recognition of national rules and accepting the rule that national specifications should be no more stringent than is required to achieve their legitimate objectives. This rule was established in the *Cassis de Dijon* judgment.

For the purpose of harmonization, the European Community has developed the 'new approach' which introduces an approach carefully balanced between government and private autonomous bodies and in which Community legislation and European standards play a distinct complementary role. Thus, instead of imposing technical solutions, Community legislation is limited to establishing the essential requirements which products must meet. Products manufactured in accordance with European standards are presumed to meet such essential requirements, but European standards are not the only way to prove such conformity. The 'new approach' works in conjunction with the 'global approach' on product certification which governs the apposition of the 'CE mark' on the product. For other products such as pharmaceuticals, chemicals, motor vehicles, and food products, Community Directives follow the traditional regulatory pattern of providing fully detailed rules.

The free movement of goods also dictates that a number of Community harmonization measures be transposed into national law. Implementation of health and safety harmonization rules is particularly important and requires the establishment of appropriate mechanisms and organizations, both for businesses and the authorities.

Two of the 'horizontal' Directives essential to smooth running of the single market are the Directive on general product safety and the Directive on liability for defective products. The regulations concerning general product safety are covered in the section on consumer protection.

The rules on agricultural products (compliance with veterinary and plant-health standards) are explained in detail in the section on agriculture.

Descriptive summary

Having liberalized its price, trade and foreign exchange regime and established basic legal and commercial rules ensuring legal security and transparency for private economic operators, Slovakia has set the foundations for free movement of goods and services. Furthermore, in compliance with the provisions of the Europe Agreement, Slovakia has made a firm commitment to trade liberalization, the abolishment of all quantitative restrictions and elimination of discriminatory measures, resulting in the creation of a free trade area by 2002. 95% of prices have been liberalized, with the remaining 5% of controlled prices applying to rents, energy and certain other household goods.

Certain technical barriers to trade have developed in relation to Slovak standards and testing procedures. Slovakia took the first step towards application of the Community's new approach to technical harmonization with the adoption of Law 142/1991 which established the basis for voluntary standardization as opposed to mandatory requirements. The Slovak Office of Standards, Metrology and Testing (UNMS), an affiliate member of the Comité Européen de Normalisation (CEN) and the Comité Européen de Normalisation Electrotechnique (Cenelec) was set up to draft and enforce legislation in this field. In 1995, however, Slovakia passed legislation which is not in complete conformity with EC legislation and practice, requiring a greater extent of pre-market testing and mandatory certification than is the case in the EU. In addition, sectoral legislation has been introduced (e.g. on food labelling and mineral water) which is not in conformity with EC legislation and could develop into technical barriers to trade.

Current and prospective assessment

Slovakia has made significant progress in liberalizing prices and trade and hence establishing the foundations for the free movement of goods. Slovakia has consistently met the deadlines established under the trade provisions of the Europe Agreement (EA) and has been actively engaged in further liberalization measures such as the adoption of new provisions on rules of origin. However, the Slovak record in complying with the balance of payments provisions of the Europe Agreement has not been optimal. On 1 may 1997 the Slovak Government introduced an import deposit scheme. These matter is presented in other parts of the opinion.

Potential constraints to free movement of goods could arise in relation to Slovak domestic legislation on prices as well as standards and testing procedures. With regard to the former, a law on prices which gives very broad powers to the Ministry of Finance and to local administrations to intervene in the domestic market for products, services, works, leases, rents and intangibles as well as the import and export of these items could represent, if ever implemented, a serious impediment to the free movement of goods.

With regard to technical legislation standards and certification, the Slovak National Programme on legislative approximation, foresees detailed implementation of White Paper measures mostly in the period 1997 to 1999, while the year 2000 is indicated as the final date for complete implementation of all remaining measures. Most new approach Directives are planned for adoption once the general legislative framework is in place.

This should be ensured by the adoption of a general act on technica requirements for products which will contain the principles of new and global approaches. Important delays have already affected the adoption of this framework legislation and the necessary accompanying legislation on product liability. Although in the automotive, pharmaceutical, foodstuffs and chemical sectors, legislative alignment is tentatively scheduled until 1999, no concrete evidence of substantive work has been made available to the Commission.

The problem of standards remaining mandatory in Slovakia is not entirely solved. The movement to the system of voluntary standards has been impeded by a lack of consensus, at national level, as to the role and scope of technical regulations and to the adoption of a system based on private responsibility rather than on a central legislative authority.

Concerning conformity assessment, a wide coverage of products is submitted to mandatory certification. This situation should be remedied through the regulatory adaptations described above and the full application of voluntary standardization.

The Slovak authorities intend to amend the current civil code to achieve full conformity with EC requirements in respect of civil liability for defective products.

In the areas subject to national rules and not covered by Community harmonization, there is not enough information available to assess whether Community legal principles on the free movement of goods are properly applied in Slovakia. The reporting procedures which form part of the internal-market machinery are not yet operational and so cannot be used in the pre-accession period. The most important instruments in this connection are: Directive 83/189, requiring governments to report draft national technical standards and regulations; Decision 3052/95 on measures derogating from the principle of the free movement of goods; procedures by which complaints can be submitted to the Commission; and Article 177 of the Treaty, enabling Member States to ask for preliminary rulings from the Court of Justice. It is also hard to assess whether Slovakia complies with the principle of mutual recognition; more information is required on its national rules, and on administrative practices, which can have an effect on product marketing.

Conclusion

Slovakia is progressively taking on the full *acquis* related to free movement of goods and has a solid record of compliance with the trade liberalization provisions of the Europe Agreement. However, the tendency to revert to balance of payments restriction measures and the slow progress in legislative alignment and in implementing a compatible system of voluntary standardization and conformity assessment reflect weaknesses in compliance with the provisions of the Europe Agreement and do not figure positively in the assessment of Slovakia's facilitation of the free movement of goods.

In the area of standards and certification, a considerable effort will be needed before a sufficiently developed situation exists for enabling a conclusion to the effect that the *acquis* will be fully and effectively implemented by Slovakia over the medium term. The Slovak authorities also need to ensure that in fields not covered by Community harmonization their own national legislation is not likely to hinder trade, in particular by checking that provisions in force are commensurate with the goals pursued. If these various elements are achieved, it is not expected that the free circulation

of goods will be a major obstacle at the point of accession.

Free movement of capital

The Europe Agreement establishes the principle of the free movement of capital between Slovakia and the EU. This, as far as the obligations of Slovakia are concerned, applies from the entry into force of the agreement as regards direct investments made by companies already established in the Slovak Republic and, as regards branches and agencies of Community companies (as well as the self employed), gradually during the transitional period. The White Paper highlights the link between the free movement of capital and the free movement of financial services. It suggests a sequence of capital movements' liberalization starting from long-term capital movements and those linked to commercial transactions to short-term capital.

Descriptive summary

The main volume of capital account inflows are accounted for by foreign loans (upwards of ECU 480 million, roughly 75% of which is of a long-term nature), followed by inward portfolio investment (mainly related to privatization and trading of securities with the Czech Republic). Foreign direct investment (FDI), the third largest category of capital inflow into Slovakia, has been modest. Between 1990 and 1995 FDI reached ECU 640 million.

The large foreign exchange inflows other than FDI have boosted foreign exchange reserves over the last two years to reach a current level of USD 3 billion. The volume of Slovak direct investments abroad is approximately SKK 200 million.

Current and prospective assessment

Slovakia has introduced full current account convertibility: the koruna was made fully convertible for current account transactions (1 October 1995) and for incoming long-term capital movements (foreign investment). The capital transactions of the banks are fully liberalized. The strategy adopted by Slovakia in implementing the White Paper in the capital movements area corresponds in general to that suggested by the White Paper by liberalizing first direct investment, credits linked to commercial transactions and inward capital movements.

However, given the good macroeconomics situation and performance of the country, a quicker pace of capital liberalization (notably regarding capital outflow) could allow a more rapid integration of Slovakia in the international economic and financial system. In the context of its OECD application, the Slovak Government announced in mid-1996 its intention to fully liberalize capital inflows in 1998, followed by capital outflows in 1999, and liberalization of remaining portfolio and overseas account restrictions in 2000.

The schedule was accelerated with the government lifting a number of capital movement restrictions already in December 1996 which authorized Slovak FDI in OECD countries (with liberalization of FDI in other countries to be authorized on 31 December 1998); enabled Slovak citizens to purchase real estate in the OECD Member States; allowed the acceptance and extension of financial credits for three or more years and the extension to financial credits for 5 or more years to OECD countries. The Slovak Government expects to liberalize fully capital movements by the year 2000.

Remaining restrictions on foreign direct investment and other capital movements include the purchase of shares in resident banks, shares of the stock exchange, real estate for non-business purposes by non-residents, auditing companies, strategic companies and to the issue or placement of securities issued by non-residents on the domestic market.

Conclusion

The Slovak Government has made a commitment both in regard to the Europe Agreement and within the OECD to an ambitious schedule of liberalization in the capital market. Europe Agreement commitments have been met and indeed exceeded in the area of inward capital movements. It can be expected that further liberalization commitments will be met as well.

Free movement of services

The basis of the free movement of services is the prohibition of discrimination, in particular on grounds of nationality, and rules on the alignment of divergent national legislation. These rules often concern both the right of establishment, which comes under the heading of the free movement of persons, and the freedom to provide services. Their implementation implies the establishment of administrative structures (banking control boards,

audio-visual control authorities, regulatory bodies) and greater cooperation between Member States in the area of enforcement (mutual recognition arrangements).

A substantial amount of the legislation applicable to the free movement of services relates to financial services. It also concerns the problems relating to the opening-up of national markets in the sectors traditionally dominated by monopolies, for example telecommunications and, to a certain extent, energy and transport. These subjects will be dealt with in the sections of the opinion specifically referring to them.

Descriptive summary

The share of the three largest banks in terms of total loans and deposits at end of March 1996 was 65% and 70% respectively. These three banks are predominantly State-owned. The participation of foreign banks increased significantly. The Banking Supervisory Authority is a department of the National Central Bank.

As a result of the first wave of voucher privatization most of the Slovak medium-sized and large enterprises are currently listed or registered on the Bratislava Stock Exchange (BSE) and the MR-system (MRS – Market registration system). The supervisory authority is for the time being the Ministry of Finance, but the setting up of an independent Securities Commission is being considered by the Slovak authorities.

The former Slovak monopoly, is the largest insurance company with 72% of the life insurance and 76% of the non life market (1996). A new insurance law was adopted in March 1991 to abolish State monopoly of the insurance industry and set up an Insurance Supervisory Authority.

Current and prospective assessment

Considerable progress has been made in adopting the *acquis* related to financial services (banks) both in terms of Stage 1 and Stage 2 measures. The first Banking Directive, the Own Funds Directive, the Deposit Guarantee Scheme, and the Solvency Ratio Directive have been approximated. The Money Laundering Directive, the Large Exposures Directive and the Second Banking Directive have been partially approximated. The latter are for the most part in conformity with the EC directives but will require changes to conform fully. For example, on money laundering, provisions of the Slovak legislation on proof of identity should include the deposits on transferable bearer passbooks.

Important Directives that have not been adopted are the Directive on the Supervision of Credit Institutions on a Consolidated Basis, the Capital Adequacy Directive, the Directive on Annual Accounts and Consolidated Accounts of Credit Institutions. The Directive concerning supervision on a consolidated basis is very important since it permits the bank supervisors to reach a global view of the risks of the individual banks and their related groups. The directive on annual accounts is important because it provides the basis for the calculation of solvency ratios on an individual and consolidated basis.

It is expected that Slovakia will be able to fully approximate EC Directives in the banking sector over the next three years. A considerable effort will be required, however, particularly in view of the high level of State ownership in the domestic banking sector and the weak financial situation of the domestic banks, related to the accumulation of 'bad debts', to adequately enforce the banking regulations. In this context the independence of the Slovak National Bank in its supervisory role will need to be further strengthened.

Although legislation (Law on Collective Investment and the Securities Law) has been adopted which largely approximates the EC Directives, further work needs to be carried out.

Adjustments needed in the legislation include provisions for a clearer definition of the environment for the listed companies, independent supervision, effective protection of minority shareholders, a definition of effective control, increased transparency on tax and fiscal implications for different groups of securities, clearer procedures for the issuance and revocation of licences, financial disclosure and the identification of major shareholders, shareholder information in conformity with the EU Directives and the prevention of insider trading. Legislation on collective investments in securities needs to be modified.

The securities market suffers from a lack of transparency and weaknesses concerning the protection of minority shareholders. Regulation of the capital markets is left to the Ministry of Finance which does not have transparent standards and criteria for decision-making, including those covering the granting and revoking of licenses. The implementation and enforcement of legislation would benefit from the creation of an independent securities commission or any other independent supervisory authority.

The Stage 1 White Paper measures on insurance have not thus far been fully approximated in Slovak Legislation. The 1991 Act on Insurance departs significantly from EC legislation although amendments approved in 1995 and 1996 have improved the situation considerably. There are still weaknesses and gaps in the legislation related to licensing and prudential supervision. In particular, provisions on basic solvency margins/technical reserves and the requirement to deposit 30% of technical reserves with domestic banking institutions are not in line with EC Directives. Concerning establishment, foreign branches are not allowed. Foreign insurance companies have to set up full subsidiaries or joint ventures. These restrictions on establishment are not fully in line with Slovakia's obligations under the Europe Agreement.

Considerable progress will have to registered if full adoption and adequate implementation of the *acquis* in the insurance sector is to be achieved over the medium term. The Slovak Government has indicated that alignment of the Insurance Act with Stage 1 measures will be accomplished in the second half of 1998. Stage 2 measures are going to be adopted at the time of Slovak accession. The Insurance Supervisory Authority is supposed to be an independent body but is in effect part of the Ministry of Finance. Its ability to effectively monitor and control the industry is weak. Finally, the ability to achieve market conditions in this sector over the medium term is questionable given the State monopolization of the industry. Only the privatization of the main State-owned insurance company will improve this situation, but it was decided at the end of 1996 that such privatization could occur only after 2003. This decision also applies to the State Saving Bank.

Conclusion

It is expected that Slovakia will be able to fully approximate EC Directives in the banking sector over the next five years. However, a considerable effort will be required to adequately enforce the legislation, particularly in regard to the remaining State-owned banks, one of which is not to be privatized before 2003.

Legislative approximation in the securities area is achievable over the medium term. The implementation and enforcement of legislation would benefit from the creation of an independent securities commission or any other supervisory authority. There is a strong commitment of the authorities to conform as soon as possible to the European requirements, but the attitude of the Parliament on privatization calls for a certain prudence on their possibility to achieve the goal.

Considerable progress will have to be registered in privatization and approximation and enforcement of legislation if Slovakia is to be able to effectively adopt and implement the *acquis* in the insurance sector. On the basis of progress to date, the prospects for full adoption of the *acquis* in this area are not positive.

Free movement of persons

The free movement of persons encompasses two concepts with different logical implications in the Treaty. On the one hand, Article 7(a) in Part One of the Treaty on 'Principles' mentions the concept in connection with the establishment of the internal market and implies that persons are not to be subject to controls when crossing the internal frontiers between the Member States. On the other hand, Article 8(a) in Part Two of the Treaty on 'Citizenship of the Union' gives every citizen of the Union the individual right to move and reside freely within the territory of the Member States, subject to certain conditions. The abolition of frontier checks must apply to all persons, whatever their nationality, if Article 7(a) is not to be meaningless. While the rights deriving from Article 8(a) apply in all Member States, those stemming from Article 7(a) have never been fully applied throughout the Union.

a) Free movement of Union citizens, freedom of establishment and mutual recognition of diplomas and qualifications

The Europe Agreement provides for the non-discriminatory treatment of workers that are legally employed (as well as their families). It covers the possibility of cumulating or transferring social security rights, and encourages Member States to conclude bilateral agreements with Slovakia on access to labour markets. During the second phase of the transitional period, the Association Council will examine further ways of improving the movement of workers.

The White Paper considers the legislative requirements in order to achieve a harmonious development of the labour market, whilst simultaneously preventing distortions of competition.

The free movement of workers is one of the fundamental freedoms enshrined in the Treaty; freedom to practise certain professions (e.g. in the legal and health fields) may, however, be subject to certain conditions, such as qualifications. Depending on the case, these may be dealt with through coordination or by applying the principle of mutual recognition. Freedom of establishment is also guaranteed under the Treaty and covers the

economic activity of self-employed natural persons and companies.

The free choice of place of residence may thus be subject to minimum conditions as to resources and health insurance where the person does not exercise a profession in the country concerned.

Descriptive summary

Slovak legislation does not impose national quotas for work permits. Current regulations require that foreign workers have a visa, a work permit and a long-term residence permit. Possession of a work permit is a necessary condition for receiving a long-term residence permit for employment purposes. If the validity of the work permit is not extended by the labour office, the validity of the residence permit expires as well. Work permits are issued for certain professions. They are issued for a period of one year maximum and are renewable. There is no limit on the employment of foreign workers as long as the situation on the labour market allows it.

The free movement of persons is closely linked to the freedom to provide services, especially those requiring minimum professional qualifications which is in turn facilitated by legislation on mutual recognition of diplomas. Part of the *acquis* (equivalence of curriculum and duration of studies for most of the professions whose training is coordinated by sectoral Directives, structures for many professions) is already taken over and full approximation is foreseen by Slovakia for 1999. In particular, training, where coordinated by Directives for seven professions, is rather broadly in line with the *acquis*, although a number of adaptations are still necessary. Enforcement structures are adequate but should be strengthened.

Integration with EU professional associations is developing well (for example engineering diplomas already meet the minimum European standards).

Current and prospective assessment

While the Slovak Republic has already adopted some measures to adopt its social legislation to EU standards, amendments to the current legislation on foreigners and on employment of foreigners will have to be adopted to bring legislation fully into line with EU principles of free movement of workers. Concerning mutual recognition of diplomas, Slovakia should be able to take up the acquis in the medium term.

Conclusion

The necessary structures to facilitate the free movement of persons seem to be in place but it is not possible at this stage to fully assess their effectiveness. Adaptation of legislation and the implementation/enforcement structures related to free movement of persons is needed if Slovakia is to fully adopt the *acquis* in this area. The achievement of these adaptations is feasible in the medium term.

b) Abolition of checks on persons at internal frontiers

The free movement of persons within the meaning of Article 7(a) of the EC Treaty, namely the abolition of checks on all persons, whatever their nationality, at the internal frontiers has not yet been fully implemented in the Union. Doing away with checks on persons is conditional on the introduction of a large number of accompanying measures, some of which have yet to be approved and implemented by the Member States (see separate section on justice and home affairs). However, that objective has been achieved by a limited number of Member States in accordance with the Schengen Convention (seven Member States already apply it and another six are working towards implementation).

The draft Treaty aims to make that objective easier to achieve within the Union by including a new chapter on an area of freedom, security and justice and incorporating the Schengen acquis into the EU.

Slovakia has indicated its desire to become a party to the Schengen Agreement and requested observer status in Schengen on the occasion of the EU-SR Association Council in February 1997. Slovakia has requested institutional and technical cooperation in regard to border controls.

General evaluation

Slovakia's progress in the implementation of legislation relating to the White Paper is summarized in the annex. According to the table, Slovakia considers that by 30 June 1997 it will have adopted national transposing legislation for 664 of the 899 Directives and Regulations in the White Paper. That figure covers legislation which Slovakia considers it will have transposed or will have checked for compatibility with Community rules and does not prejudge actual compatibility as such, on which the Commission is not able at this stage to state an opinion.

Significant progress towards legislative alignment has been achieved in the important areas of company law, banking, securities and free movement of capital. In these fields, most measures have been transposed according to an assessment carried out by the Slovak authorities, but the Commission is not able to say if they are fully compatible with Community law.

Further work will nevertheless be necessary in these areas to achieve full alignment with Community requirements. In the fields of standards and certification, industrial and intellectual property (in particular copyright), public procurement and insurance, however, more considerable efforts will have to be made if Slovakia is to achieve full alignment with Community legislation in the medium term.

Despite the efforts undertaken, real progress in transposing very recently adopted legislation still has to be reinforced by detailed implementing rules and the establishment of an efficient administrative structure. Slovakia possesses some infrastructure which functions fairly well, but major efforts still need to be made in several fields, especially standardization and the technical structures required to implement the 'new approach', as well as in the areas of public procurement and industrial and intellectual property.

The Commission cannot, at this stage, give an opinion on the ability of businesses, especially small and medium-sized businesses, to implement the *acquis*.

Leaving aside certain specific aspects relating to agriculture, checks at the internal frontiers of the Union can only be abolished once sufficient legislative harmonization has been achieved. This calls for mutual confidence, based in particular on sound administration (for example the importance of safety checks on some products at the place of departure). As far as goods are concerned, the completion of the internal market on 1 January 1993 was only achieved by doing away with all the formalities and checks performed by the Member States at the internal borders of the Union. In particular these checks covered technical points (product safety), veterinary, animal-health and plant-health matters, economic and commercial matters (for example prevention of counterfeiting of goods), security (weapons, etc.) and environmental aspects (waste, etc.).

In most cases, the abolition of checks was only made possible by the adoption and application of Community measures harmonizing the rules on movement and placement on the market (particularly as regards product safety) and, where applicable, by shifting the place where controls and formalities within the Member States or on their markets are conducted (in particular as regards VAT and excise duties, veterinary and plant-health checks, and the collection of statistics). A section of Slovakia's present borders will become the Union's external frontier and this means border checks will need to be stepped up (see separate sections on customs).

In view of the overall assessment that can be made of progress achieved to date and the rate at which work is advancing in the various areas concerned, it is difficult at present to put a time-scale on Slovakia's ability to take over and implement all the instruments required to abolish internal border checks and to transfer those checks to the Union's external frontier.

Slovakia has already adopted significant elements of the *acquis* relating to the single market. However, the Commission is not yet able to take a position on every measure whose transposition has been reported by Slovakia. Further progress will be needed with regard notably to standards and certification, public procurement and intellectual property. In most areas, enforcement needs to be strengthened. A particular effort will be necessary with regard to the strengthening of the administration. In the medium term, provided current efforts are stepped up, Slovakia can be expected to have adopted and implemented most of the single market legislation and made the necessary progress on the mechanisms of enforcement, in order to be able to participate fully in the internal market.

Competition

European Community competition policy derives from Article 3 (g) of the Treaty providing that the Community shall have 'a system ensuring that competition in the internal market is not distorted'. The main areas of application are anti-trust and State aid.

The Europe Agreement provides for a competition regime to be applied for trade relations between the Community and Slovakia based on the criteria of Articles 85 and 86 of the EC Treaty (agreements between undertakings/abuses of dominant position) and in Article 92 (State aid) and for implementing rules in these fields to be adopted within three years of the entry into force of the agreement. Furthermore it provides that Slovakia will make its legislation compatible with that of the Community in the field of competition.

The White Paper refers to the progressive application of the above provisions and those of the Merger Regulation (4064/89) and of Articles 37 and 90 (monopolies and special rights).

Descriptive summary

Slovakia has moved quickly to establish a legislative and institutional framework compatible with that of the European Union while at the same time proceeding with privatization so as to reduce the role of the State in the economy. However, continued public monopolies, extensive public ownership through the National Property Fund and the existence of anti-competitive price fixing legislation remain important factors in assessing the competition environment.

The National Council of the Slovak Republic adopted on 8 July 1994, the 'Act on Protection of Economic Competition'. The purpose of the act is to protect economic competition in the markets for products and services against prevention, restriction or distortion as well as to create conditions for its further development, in order to promote economic progress for the benefit of consumers. The Anti-monopoly Office (AMO) was set up as the central administrative organ, responsible for the enforcement of the anti-trust law.

With regard to public undertakings and undertakings with special or exclusive rights, the Slovak Government's privatization policy has excluded 29 essential companies, with a combined book value of 100 billion SKK, from the privatization process. These enterprises are mainly in the energy sector, post and telecommunications, transport, the armaments sector, water management, insurance and banking. The Slovak Government has maintained a veto in 12 additional, so-called strategic, enterprises.

The responsibility for monitoring State aid is vested with a department under the Ministry of Finance. No specific rules have been established for the functioning of the monitoring authority on State aid to define its powers to collect information and adopt opinions or decisions on the compatibility of State aid with the Europe Agreement.

A first report on existing State aid has been made covering the period 1993-1994.

Current and prospective assessment

In the field of anti-trust the current legislation fulfils to a large degree the requirements in terms of approximation of legislation. Only a few adjustments need to be made in the area of block exemptions, merger control and procedures.

As concerns public undertakings and undertakings with special exclusive rights, the 29 'essential enterprises' excluded from privatization and the remaining 12 'strategic enterprises' in which the State maintains a veto right are exempt from the application of bankruptcy legislation. Considerable progress will be needed to make these enterprises commercially viable through restructuring and to liberalize the sectors in which some of these essential enterprises operate (e.g. telecommunications, transport, energy, postal services).

No specific rules on the functioning of the monitoring authority on State aid within the Ministry of Finance have been adopted yet. It remains unclear what are the powers of the monitoring authority to control State aid and it seems clear that under the present system it is not possible for the monitoring authority to collect all information necessary from all aid granting authorities to examine the compatibility of State aid with the Europe Agreement.

The transparency in the field of State aid has not achieved the level required. A first aid inventory for State aid granted in 1993-1994 has been established which does not, however, provide the information necessary to see who benefits from State aid and for what purpose State aid is granted.

Certain aid measures seem to be contingent upon export performance which is clearly not compatible with the Europe Agreement and an important part of State aid seems to be granted through indirect forms of State aid, such as tax reliefs, debt write-offs and tax arrears. These aid measures constitute operating aid which are only allowed under very strict conditions. Due to the lack of transparency it is as yet unclear whether the conditions for granting operating aid are complied with. The adoption of the draft revitalisation act would aggravate further the situation.

In addition to the adoption of legislation sufficiently approximate to that of the EC, credible enforcement of competition law requires the establishment of well functioning anti-trust and State aid monitoring authorities. It requires moreover that the judicial system, the public administration and the relevant economic operators have a sufficient understanding of competition law and policy.

Conclusion

Approximation of legislation in the field of anti-trust is progressing satisfactorily and will be in place in

the medium term. Moreover, the Anti-monopoly Office seems to have the skills and resources necessary to enforce the law. However, the most important challenge will be to ensure that the law applies to all undertakings, including the so-called essential and strategic enterprises.

In the field of State aid much work lies ahead, in particular to establish the necessary transparency, to bring into line with the Europe Agreement the existing State aid measures and to adopt the rules for the efficient functioning of the monitoring authority on State aid. In particular, the aid inventory should cover all measures granted by the State, regional or local authorities or through State resources. The rules on State aid should apply to all undertakings, including the so-called essential and strategic companies. A considerable effort will be necessary to fulfil the requirements in the field of State aid control over the medium term.

3.2. Innovation

Information society

Present situation

The economic and social effects made possible by the combination of information technology and telecommunications are great. In Slovakia these possibilities were neglected before 1989 although education generally was not. The result seems to be that demand for computers has spurted beyond normal expectation deduced from GDP per capita. The number of host computers on the Internet (1.6 per 1 000 inhabitants in January 1997), as a relative measure of development towards the information society (IS), is growing very fast although Slovakia is about average for the region and has not yet reached the position which the average EU country reached two years ago. The ongoing modernization of the telecommunications network should soon begin to boost the volume of data transmission, including for the Internet.

Conclusion

The size of the market for information technology (IT) products is an encouraging sign of rising potential in Slovakia for IS related activities. A more liberal approach to new entrants to the data services market might have a positive effect but the key stimulus will probably be the more general availability of advanced services.

Education, training and youth

Articles 126 and 127 of the EC Treaty provide that the Community shall contribute to the development of quality education and implement a vocational training policy aimed at promoting the European dimension in education and at enhancing industrial adaptation and the responsiveness of the labour market through vocational training policies.

The Europe Agreement provides for cooperation in raising the level of education and professional qualifications. The White Paper includes no measures in this field.

Descriptive summary

Slovakia's spending on education amounts to 1.5% of GDP. It takes 3.2% of the State budget.

There are 1 150 000 pupils, 72 500 students and 82 500 teachers in Slovakia.

The Slovak education system is composed of primary, secondary and higher education, including vocational educational training. Education reforms undertaken since 1989 in the primary and secondary education fields have included the authorization of private education, increased autonomy for school principals and local and regional authorities, curricula reform and an increase in the duration of obligatory school education. There are 14 higher education institutions in Slovakia (including three for teacher training), two military colleges and one police academy, all of which are financed by the government.

A Council of Higher Education was established in 1990 to represent the higher education institutions in their dealings with the Ministry of Education. The Higher Education Act of 1990 which granted a high degree of autonomy to academic institutions was amended in 1996. The amendments were generally perceived as significantly increasing the influence of the Ministry of Education and encroaching on academic freedom. A new vocational education and training system is being developed.

Tempus has contributed to the goals of achievement of higher education reform and created the basis for cooperation with EU higher education institutes.

About 16.5% of the total Slovak population is aged between 15 and 25. Slovak youth institutions have been involved in European Youth activities since 1990. From 1995 on, youth cooperation with Slovakia has also been included in the Youth for Europe programme.

Current and prospective assessment

In compliance with the Europe Agreement, cooperation with Slovakia having the aim of raising the level of general education and professional qualifications has been established and the participation of the Slovak Republic in Community programmes in these areas is imminent.

Further reforms are envisaged, aiming at qualitative improvement of the Slovak education system at all levels. Teacher training will be an important component of those reforms. With a view to the adaptation of the work force to the ongoing process of economic restructuring, and given the need to ensure compatibility of standards with those in the EU Member States, continued reform of the vocational education system is of crucial importance.

Provided that reforms proceed as foreseen, the Slovak education and training sector should be fully able to participate in cooperative actions within the European Union.

Conclusion

In the perspective of accession, no major problems should be expected in these fields.

Research and technological development

Research and technological development activities at Community level, as provided for by the Treaty and in the framework programme, aim at improving the competitiveness of European industry, the quality of life, as well as supporting sustainable development, environmental protection, and other common policies.

The Europe Agreement and its additional protocol provides for cooperation in these areas, notably through participation in the framework programme. The White Paper includes no measures in this field.

Descriptive summary

The main responsibility for the development, coordination and implementation of the national science and technology policy, which was with the Office for Strategy of the Development of Society, Science and Technology of the Slovak Republic since 1995, was moved back to the Ministry of Education at the beginning of 1997. The most important grant agency is still attached to the above-mentioned office and operates on the principle of general tenders, open to researchers of all institutional backgrounds. The Slovak Academy of Sciences, the 14 Slovak universities and the applied research institutes are the main actors in the science and technology field.

Total expenditure fell from 2.25% of GDP in 1991 to 1.04% in 1995 and public expenditure from 0.71% of GDP in 1991 to 0.37% in 1994, but public expenditure has since increased to 0.51% in 1996.

The general priorities of the government in this sector are: to establish an effective system of State support, and to increase the share of science and technology in the State budget expenditure to 1% of GDP. Priority subjects are: reducing raw-material requirements, increasing energy efficiency, optimizing the agro-ecosystems.

Regular cooperation with the European Community started in 1992 with the third research and technology development framework programme. So far, cooperation was mainly concentrated on Copernicus (specific programme for cooperation with CECs and NIS) and remains rather low for participation in the fourth framework programme. Slovakia is a member of COST (European cooperation in the field of scientific and technical research) and Eureka (European Research Coordination Agency).

Since 1994, the statistics in this sector are compatible with OECD standards.

Current and prospective assessment

Slovakia disposes of a high level research and development sector which, due to substantial reductions in government support, has been rapidly rationalized. The legal and financial framework for research and development now needs to be consolidated in order to stabilize the sector and give it a clear perspective for future development. Draft legislation on research and development is in preparation. Funding should be increased and become more diversified.

Increased participation in Community programmes should help consolidate this sector and better serve the industrial innovation.

Conclusion

In the perspective of accession, no major problems should be expected in this field. Accession would be of mutual benefit.

Telecommunications

The objectives of EC telecommunications policy are the elimination of obstacles to the effective operation of the single market in telecommunications equipment, services and networks, the opening of foreign markets to EU companies and the achievement of universally available modern services for EU residents and businesses. These are achieved through harmonization of the standards and conditions for services offering the liberalization of the markets for terminals, services and networks and the adoption of necessary regulatory instruments. The Directives and policies needed to achieve this have now been established, but the liberalization of public voice telephony and operation of related infrastructure will be deferred for a year or two after 1998 in certain Member States.

The Europe Agreement provides for cooperation aimed at enhancing standards and practices towards EC levels in telecommunication and postal policies, standardization, regulatory approaches and the modernization of infrastructure. The White Paper focuses on the approximation of regulation, networks and services, followed by further steps ensuring gradual sector liberalization.

Descriptive summary

Telephone availability has increased to 23.2 per 100 inhabitants at the end of 1996. At the end of 1996 there were 145 000 unsatisfied requests for telephone services. The government aims to reduce the waiting time for a telephone line to five months by the year 2000 and to have 35 lines per 100 by that date.

The majority of telecommunications services are provided by Slovenske telekomunikacie (ST) which is a State monopoly. Its transformation into a joint stock company is currently under preparation. The government has recognized that private sector capital will be needed to continue expansion of the sector and is considering options for privatization of ST.

Current and prospective assessment

Degree of liberalization

The government has undertaken in the WTO negotiations to liberalize the remaining monopoly held by Slovenske Telecom (ST) on voice telephony by 1 January 2003. There is liberalization in all other services except alternative infrastructures and there is competition except in paging where ST has recently merged with the only paging company which had

French and Czech companies as partners. Until 1997 there was only one mobile operator (analogue) but two new mobile networks working to the new pan-European digital standard (GSM) came into service in 1996.

Approximation to EC Law

The Telecommunications Act of 1964 was amended in 1992 (by the former federal government) so as to separate regulatory functions from operational ones. The changes also abolished the statutory monopolies, permitted privatization, imposed licensing requirements on existing operators and thereby empowered the government to adopt a policy of liberalization which, however, it has yet to do. A more effective separation of the regulatory and policy body from any operating company will be necessary to comply with the acquis and to enable the government to administer a pro-competitive policy successfully.

New telecommunications legislation is due in 1997 to prepare for the privatization of ST. This new legislation, currently in draft form, provides for the division of regulatory activities between four entities: the Ministry of Transport and Communications, the Telecommunications Office, the Regional Telecommunications Offices and the Ministry of Finance which will regulate some tariffs. Since independence, progress on passing new legislation in the sector has been slow and there seems to be insufficient administrative capacity to meet the targets adopted.

Tariff rebalancing is in hand although pricing policy is complicated by the division of powers between two ministries. As the main network expands into areas that are less economically vigorous, policy measures will be needed if universal service is to be achieved.

Infrastructure

The government's principal objective has been to boost investment in the expansion and modernization of the public telecommunications networks and to improve the quality of services available. Much expansion has taken place so far on the basis of internally generated profits and on loans from the international financing institutions and as the long distance network reaches completion, the availability of advanced services, especially in cities, will greatly improve. Between 1991 and 1996 the fixed network grew from 14.3 to 23.5 lines per 100 inhabitants compared to the average of 43.9 for

Greece, Portugal and Ireland. The government aims to reduce the waiting time for a telephone line to five months by the year 2000 and to have 35 lines per 100 inhabitants by that date. Provided that the government can finance the investment, this target may be achievable. The digitization rate of the public network is 38% compared to an average of 62.4% for Greece, Portugal and Ireland.

The government is considering options for privatization of ST as a further means to obtain finance for investment. The current revenue per line may be too low to achieve universal service. The level of purchasing power would suggest that further tariff reform could produce more revenue. At the end of 1996 there were only 25 000 cellular mobiles, that is 0.47 per 100 inhabitants.

Competitiveness of the sector

In 1995, there were 13.7 employees per 1 000 lines compared to the average of 6.2 for Greece, Portugal and Ireland and new subscribers had waited on average 1.5 years for their lines. There is a large number of unsatisfied requests for telephone services and even at today's high rate of network expansion, it will be a few years more before even a basic telephone service will be universally available. Revenue per line (about ECU 264 p.a. in 1995) is close to the lower limit needed to ensure that the network can be run as a profitable business while supplying affordable universal service. Efficiency savings by the public operator are necessary if it is to be competitive. Provided that tariff rebalancing is continued and the economy continues to grow, the telecommunications services sector should be able to face full liberalization when it comes in 2003.

Conclusion

Slovakia will have some difficulty in complying with the *acquis communautaire* in the medium term because there is insufficient administrative capacity to complete new legislation and enforce it. Greater competitiveness of the public operator must be achieved to attract investment and to prepare for competition.

Audio-visual

The audio-visual *acquis* aims, in the context of the internal market, at the provision and free movement of audio-visual services within the EU as well as the promotion of the European programme industry.

The Television without Frontiers Directive, which is applicable to all broadcasters regardless of the modes of transmission (terrestrial, satellite, cable) or their private or public nature, contains this acquis, setting down basic rules concerning transfrontier broadcasting. The main points are: to ensure the free movement of television broadcasts throughout member states; to promote the production and distribution of European audio-visual works (by laying down a minimum proportion of broadcasting time for European works and those by independent producers); to set basic standards in the field of television advertising; to provide for the protection of minors and to allow for the right of reply.

The Europe Agreement provides for cooperation in the promotion and modernization of the audio-visual industry, and the harmonization of regulatory aspects of audio-visual policy.

The Television without Frontiers Directive is a Stage I measure in the White Paper.

Descriptive summary

The legal framework for the audio-visual sector is determined by the 1991 Slovak Television Act, and the 1991 Radio and Television Broadcasting Act. The first act dismantles the State's monopoly and prescribes the basic rules, rights and regulations for broadcasting and broadcasters, whilst the latter provides for the Radio and Television Broadcasting Council, which decides on licences granted to broadcasters.

The main television broadcaster is Slovak Television.

Since the State monopoly over film production and distribution was lifted, small private producers have become active. The distribution sector is occupied by several companies.

Current and prospective assessment

The audio-visual sector in Slovakia is attempting to re-establish itself after major upheavals in recent years, and is characterized by rapid growth and constant change. Its ability to properly adhere to the *acquis* presupposes an upgrading of the capacity of the programme-making industry to meet the important challenges of an adapted regulatory framework.

Slovak audio-visual legislation is not fully compatible with EU requirements; deficiencies remain over the promotion of European works, independent producers and recent works, the definition of European works, isolated advertising spots and the contents of advertising.

Amendments to the legislation are under discussion within the Slovak administration.

Conclusion

More complete information is required on the evolving legislative situation. However, provided that the necessary legislative measures are pursued with sufficient urgency and are accompanied by the necessary structural adaptations of the industry, it is reasonable to expect that Slovakia should be able to meet EC requirements in the audio-visual sector in the medium term.

3.3. Economic and fiscal affairs

Economic and monetary union

By the time of Slovakia's accession, the third stage of EMU will have commenced. This will mark important changes for all Member States, including those that do not participate in the euro area. All Member States, including the new ones, will participate fully in the economic and monetary union. Their economic policies will be a matter of common concern and they will be involved in the coordination of economic policies (national convergence programmes, broad economic guidelines, multilateral surveillance, excessive deficit procedure). They will be required to respect the stability and growth pact, to renounce any direct central bank financing of the public sector deficit and privileged access of public authorities to financial institutions, and to have completed the liberalization of capital movements.

Accession means closer monetary and exchange rate cooperation with the European Union. This will require strengthening structural reforms in the area of monetary and exchange rate policies. Member States not participating in the euro area will be able to conduct an autonomous monetary policy and participate in the European System of Central Banks (ESCB) on a restricted basis. Their central banks have to be independent and have price stability as their primary objective. Monetary policy has to be conducted with market-based instruments and has to be 'efficient' in transmitting its impulses to the real economy. Therefore, reforms need to be pursued to tackle factors that hinder the efficiency of monetary policy, such as the lack of competition in the banking sector, the lack of development of financial markets and the problem of 'bad loans' in the banking sector. Finally all Member States shall treat their exchange rate policy as a matter of common interest and be in a position to stabilize their exchange rates in a mechanism yet to be decided.

As membership of the European Union implies acceptance of the goal of EMU, the convergence criteria will have to be fulfilled by Slovakia, although not necessarily on accession. While the fulfilment of the convergence criteria is not a precondition for EU membership, they remain key points of reference for stability-oriented macroeconomic policies, and must in time be fulfilled by new Member States on a permanent basis. Hence the successful conclusion of systematic transformation and market-oriented structural reforms is essential. Slovakia's economic situation and progress has already been analysed in preceding chapters of this opinion.

Current and prospective assessment

The Slovak Central Bank is largely independent from the government in terms of the appointment procedure of its governor and the conduct of monetary policy. The statutory objective of the Central Bank is to ensure the stability of the Slovak currency, but it has always been interpreted in terms of price stability. The provisions of the Law on the Central Bank are still far from compatible with the Treaty, but the Slovak Republic has a sound fiscal record which has implied no budget deficit financing to date.

Monetary policy has been quite effective in driving inflation down to single digit levels, although it must be stressed that the Slovak Central Bank started to use market-oriented instruments only in 1996. The control of money supply has been relatively difficult in the past due to the combination of a fixed exchange rate and the expectation of positive real interest rates (due to low inflation). The Central Bank reacted in 1996 by widening the fluctuation margins of the exchange rate around the central parity, increasing the reserve requirements and introducing limits on the volume of refinancing credits to the banks. This has caused severe liquidity shortages in the interbank market, where there is only one supplier of deposits. Consequently, interbank interest rates are relatively high. The efficiency of monetary policy is hindered by an uncompetitive, State-dominated banking sector, that is also burdened by a substantial amount of

bad loans. In addition, the bankruptcy procedures are not effectively enforced and financial markets are relatively underdeveloped.

The exchange rate regime is a peg with fluctuation bands around the central parity. In an effort to curb the domestic external borrowing which was endangering its ability to control money supply growth, in 1996 the Slovak Central Bank progressively widened the fluctuation margins of the exchange rate around the central parity. Since 1993, the exchange rate has been stable within the targeted range.

Conclusion

It is premature to judge whether the Slovak Republic will be in a position, by the time of its accession, to participate in the euro area; that will depend on the success of its structural transformation permitting to attain and to adhere permanently to the convergence criteria, which are not however a condition of accession.

The Slovak Republic's participation in the third stage of EMU as a non-participant in the euro area should pose no problems in the medium term, provided that Central Bank legislation is made fully compatible with EC rules and that the banking sector is restructured, according to the criteria of a market economy.

Taxation

The *acquis* in the area of direct taxation mainly concerns some aspects of corporation taxes and capital duty. The four freedoms of the EC Treaty have a wider impact on national tax systems.

The indirect taxation *acquis* consists primarily of harmonized legislation in the field of value-added tax and excise duties. This includes the application of a non-cumulative general tax on consumption (VAT) which is levied on all stages of production and distribution of goods and services. This implies an equal tax treatment of domestic and non-domestic (import) transactions. The VAT acquis also contains transitional arrangements for the taxation of transactions within the European Union between taxable persons. In the field of excise duties the *acquis* contains harmonized tax structures and minimum rates of duty together with common rules on the holding and movement of harmonized excisable goods (including the use of fiscal warehouses). As a result of the introduction of the single market, all fiscal controls at the Community's internal frontiers were abolished in January 1993.

The mutual assistance between Member State tax authorities is an important feature of administrative cooperation in the internal market; the respective directive covers both direct and indirect taxation.

The Europe Agreement contains provisions on approximation of legislation in the area of indirect taxation.

The White Paper contains as Stage I measures those which make up the main requirements of the indirect taxation *acquis* (essentially, those measures applied in the Community up to 1993), and as Stage II measures those which are, in addition, necessary to implement the full indirect taxation *acquis*.

Descriptive summary

Direct taxation

The two company taxation directives and the Arbitration Convention provide for a mechanism which applies on the basis of reciprocity. Respective provisions can therefore by definition not be expected to exist before accession.

Indirect taxation

The overall contribution of VAT and excise duty revenue to the Slovak State budget was about 32% and 12% respectively in 1995. This is expected to continue on an upward trend.

Value-added tax

The current Slovak VAT system was introduced on 1 January 1993 replacing the previous single-stage turnover tax. Slovakia applies a dual VAT rate system: a standard VAT rate of 23% and a reduced VAT rate of 6%. The standard rate applies in principle to all supplies of goods and services, which are not specifically taxed at the reduced rate. As regards imports the rate applicable is the same as for similar domestically produced supplies.

Certain activities are exempt from VAT without the right to claim the input credit on such supplies. These exemptions relate mainly to activities in the public interest, financial and insurance services, and lotteries and similar games. Taxable persons are in principle, entitled to deduct VAT incurred on their purchases for business purposes of goods and services. However, the Slovakian VAT Act does not contain any provisions enabling tax to be refunded to taxable persons not established within the country.

Excise

The current system of excise duty in the Slovak Republic was introduced on 1 January 1993. Excise duties are applicable to mineral oils, alcohol and alcoholic beverages and manufactured tobacco. For each product category, the duty is specific in nature.

Mutual assistance

The tax administration has not yet had to develop its capacity for mutual assistance with the tax authorities of Member States, since mutual assistance is a feature which would only become applicable on accession.

Current and prospective assessment

Value-added tax

The current VAT system in Slovakia has been based on the main principles of the VAT legislation of the Community. It is a good starting point in its future alignment with the Community VAT *acquis*, although it is relatively general in its application.

Foreign traders who are not permanently established in Slovakia and listed in the Commercial Register cannot be registered for VAT in the country. Since Slovakia does not operate any arrangements for the refund of VAT to non-registered foreign taxable persons, VAT represents an increased cost to such traders. The application of the reduced VAT rate is notably broader in scope compared to the Community approach.

The Slovak Republic's membership of the European Union would require additional adjustments to bring the VAT legislation into line with the requirements of the Community acquis, in particular as regards the system of taxation necessary in a Community with no internal frontier controls.

The Slovak national strategy plan for implementing the recommendations of the White Paper regarding VAT initially gives priority to restructuring the VAT rate scheme, and to the tax exempt treatment of supplies of goods to foreign air and shipping companies and supplies of services rendered on board such aircraft and ships. During the period 1998 to 2000 the legislative programme is planned to focus on arrangements for the refund of VAT to taxable persons not established in Slovakia, the definition of taxable persons, and tax exemptions applicable to the temporary importation of goods other than means of transport. It is intended to fully align the

Slovak VAT legislation to that of the Community by 2000 with the exception of the Community's transitional provisions.

Excise

There are significant discrepancies between the Slovak excise regime and EU requirements.

Firstly, there exists no excise suspension system where goods can move between authorized tax warehouses without payment of duty.

Secondly, although the level of tax rates broadly oscillates around the minimum rates specified by individual EC directives, the level of rates applicable to mineral oils are below the EC minimum level, while the current specific rate of duty on cigarettes will have to be switched to a compound rate applied in the Community which consists of a specific element and an *ad valorem* element.

In order to ensure a correct application of the Community excise legislation it is essential that the Slovak Republic sets up a warehousing system based on the Community model as soon as possible, and adapts the structure and level of its excise rates in such a way that they comply with Community requirements.

The Slovak national strategy plan for implementing the recommendations of the White Paper does not provide a clear and detailed timetable for future adjustments of the Slovak excise legislation. A short-term objective consists of an approximation of Slovak excise legislation towards the Community legislation in the period 1999 to 2000. However, the effective setting-up of tax warehouses as well as the harmonization of the structure of duty on alcoholic beverages would be delayed. Accordingly, a full harmonization of the legislation is not envisaged for a further few years.

Mutual assistance

There would also be a need, on accession, to implement the appropriate arrangements for administrative cooperation and mutual assistance between Member States. These requirements are essential for the functioning of the internal market.

Conclusion

The *acquis* in respect of direct taxation should present no significant difficulties.

As regards indirect taxation, provided a sustained effort is made, the Slovak Republic should be able to comply with the *acquis* concerning VAT and excise duties in the medium term.

It should be possible to start participating in mutual assistance as the tax administration develops its expertise in this respect.

Statistics

The main principles of the Community *acquis* relate to the impartiality, reliability, transparency, confidentiality (of individual information) and dissemination of official statistics. In addition there exists an important body of principles and practices concerning the use of European and international classifications, systems of national accounts, business registers, and various categories of statistics.

The Europe Agreement provides for cooperation to develop effective and reliable statistics, in harmony with international standards and classifications.

The White Paper includes no provisions in this field.

Descriptive summary

The Statistical Office of the Slovak Republic (SOSR) is the central body charged with producing and disseminating official statistics in Slovakia. It is guided by a Statistical Council of representatives from other government administrations and from the private sector.

The legal basis for Slovak official statistics consists of the Law on State Statistics.

Current and prospective assessment

Slovak legislation is, with a few exceptions, comparable with the current standards applied within the European Union.

Some issues of transparency, confidentiality and dissemination need attention, and there are deficiencies in sectors such as national and regional accounts, and the business register. Improvements are also needed in the regional statistical system following the reform of the territorial division of the country.

Conclusion

Provided that continuing progress is made, Slovakia should be able to comply with EU requirements for official statistics within the next few years.

3.4. Sectoral policies

Industry

EC industrial policy seeks to enhance competitiveness, thus achieving rising living standards and high rates of employment. It aims at speeding up adjustment to structural change, encouraging an environment favourable to initiative, to the development of undertakings throughout the Community, and to industrial cooperation, and fostering better exploitation of the industrial potential of policies of innovation, research and technological development. EC industrial policy is horizontal by nature. Sectoral communications aim at transposing horizontal concepts into specific sectors. EC industrial policy results from an articulation of instruments from a number of Community policies; it includes both instruments related to the operation of markets (product specification and market access, trade policy, State aids and competitions policy) and measures related to industry's capacity to adapt to change (stable macroeconomic environment, technology, training, etc.).

In order to cope with competitive pressure and market forces within the Union, the industry of applicant countries needs to have achieved a certain level of competitiveness by the time of accession. The governments of applicant countries need to be seen as pursuing policies aimed at open and competitive markets along the lines set out in Article 130 ('Industry') of the Treaty. Cooperation between the EU and the candidate countries in the fields of industrial cooperation, investment, industrial standardization and conformity assessment as provided for in the Europe Agreement is also an important indicator of development in the right direction.

Descriptive summary

Until World War II Slovakia was a predominantly rural country. Its subsequent industrialization followed the imperatives of central planning with little regard to factor endowments or locational costs. As part of the CSSR in the period leading up to 1990 the country had become one of the most centrally-planned economies. The structure of the economy

Slovak industry – main production sectors in 1995

Sector	%-share industrial value-added	%-share industrial employment	%-share industrial exports
Mechanical engineering (including pressure equipment, medical apparatus, metrological equipment)	10.5	25.0	7.5
Chemicals	14.5	9.5	24.0
Metallurgy	9.0	5.5	20.0
Agri-food	8.5	9.5	2.5
Wood, cellulose, paper	7.0	8.0	8.5
Textiles/clothing, leather/shoes	5.5	15.0	5.5
Automotive industry	5.0	1.5	5.5
Electrical engineering (including consumer electr., components, telecom, office equipment)	2.0	4.0	3.0
Pharmaceuticals	2.0	1.0	2.5
Total of the above	67.5	83.0	79.0
Other industries	32.5	17.0	21.0
Total industries	100.0	100.0	100.0
Industrial production as % GDP	*32.0*	*27.0*	
Construction	*5.0*	*5.0*	
Total industry and construction	*37.0*	*32.0*	

was dominated by heavy industry (notably basic industries), which provided to a large extent inputs (steel, paper, petrochemicals) for the Czech industry.

The collapse of traditional markets and increased competition has led to industrial restructuring and a strong decline in industrial production. From 1990 to 1995 the share of industrial production (including construction) in GDP dropped by a third to 37% and stood at about ECU 5 billion. Total industrial employment fell as well and now stands at about 650 000 or 35% of the total workforce. Small firms account for three quarters of all industrial firms and for 25% of total employment while the rest, medium-sized and large firms, provide the largest share in employment. The major industries are now mechanical engineering, chemicals, metallurgy, agri-food, wood and textiles and clothing.

Engineering has remained an important sector despite a strong decline in production. The main focus of the engineering industry is the production of highway and heavy-duty construction machinery, transport equipment and hydraulics. Most firms have been privatized and the restructuring forced the exit of a number of public firms. Nevertheless, production technologies and capital stock remain obsolete and capacity utilization rates low, while modernization is impeded by lack of resources.

The chemicals industry has been a traditional leader in the Slovak economy for decades and seems competitive. The sector currently operates on a capacity utilization rate of over 80% and trades actively, mainly to the Czech Republic and the EU. Privatization remains to be carried out for 'strategic enterprises'.

The steel sector basically consists of a single large steel company. Both it and the non-ferrous metal sector are technically advanced and competitive but modernization took place without capacity reduction.

The agri-food industry is an important industrial sector. Capacity utilization rates in the industry vary widely.

The base industries wood and paper, cement, glass and ceramics are important industries as well. Generally the forest-based industries in Slovakia are less developed but opportunities exist for some sectors (e.g. wood panels) and the close proximity of Slovakia to the EU helps exports. The relatively high export and capacity utilization ratios suggest that these industries so far have been able to compete on the international markets, but the low imports together with a number of trade restrictions for some of the sectors could indicate barriers to entry for foreign exporters, like the import certification system for ceramics.

The relatively large textiles, clothing, leather and shoes sector is still in crisis. Competition with Asian manufacturers and a general lack of restructuring plague the industry, but exports still account for most of production and there is a trade surplus. To increase competitiveness, manufacturers are attempting to target new markets, upgrade production for EU markets and establish outward processing trade (OPT) links with EU manufacturers. The automotive sector is among the more dynamic sectors in manufacturing. There are two vehicle producers, one fully owned by a major German producer, and nearly all of the production is destined for the EU market. It has moved production from Germany to Bratislava to benefit from low labour costs and to develop the high quality plant into a key assembly point for niche automobiles marketed in Europe. The components industry is only slowly recovering from the break-up of Czechoslovakia. Slovak component manufacturers cooperate with a Czech car maker and the number of joint ventures with western partners is growing. The pharmaceutical industry is relatively small. Most production in 1995 was exported, almost entirely to the Czech Republic. However, exports are increasingly targeted towards western markets though it consists mainly of raw materials. Nevertheless, the production system needs restructuring and the industry is attempting to move towards western standards but resources remain scarce. In addition, a lack of funds for R&D hinders future development. The industry does not seem to have been successful in attracting foreign partners or investment, possibly also due to lack of patent protection. The pressure and metrological equipment industries are mostly small-scale. For 1995, exports greatly exceeded imports but the low capacity utilization rate does suggest a need for further restructuring. Information technology industry production facilities and methods are mostly old and obsolete. Privatization and restructuring have led to a sharp drop in production and the exit of numerous firms, despite a relatively dynamic demand growth. Those that are left need further modernization. Despite the industry decline parts of the research environment are still maintained by the State and provide a potential for new development. On the other hand, Slovak software suppliers have successfully established links with foreign clients.

The privatization process has made progress. It was carried out first through a voucher method followed by direct sales/management buy-outs, bringing the private sector share in GNP to 70%. Since 1995, however, privatization of many large companies benefited corporate and political insiders and was done in a less than transparent fashion which led to little revenue for the public authorities and few if any new capital and management input for the privatized firms. The government nevertheless maintains a controlling share in a number of 'essential and strategic companies'. These include enterprises in energy, utilities, armaments, posts and telecommunications, railways, pharmaceuticals and agro-industry. These enterprises are exempt from the application of bankruptcy legislation.

Current and prospective assessment

So far industry has developed satisfactorily despite the precarious political situation mainly because the macroeconomic environment has remained stable and the open trade regime provided for enough competition. But the outlook for industry cannot be divorced from political developments because privatization is still far from being complete and what has taken place so far has often been linked to the current regime. It thus remains to be seen whether industries that have been put in 'politically friendly' hands will in future behave competitively. This problem will be particularly acute in a number of sectors that are dominated by a single firm.

The share of investment in GDP is the highest among the associated States (almost 36%, close to that of some fast growing Asian economies).

The main problems for industry come from the lack of competitive privatization and the excessive reliance on energy intensive sectors. The State-owned firms will have less problems of access to long-term financing and thus have an advantage over the private sector in capital intensive areas. This could lead to a development similar to that experienced by some southern European Member States in the 1970s and 1980s that built up or maintained heavy capital intensive industries in State hands despite mounting losses. A development in this direction would greatly diminish the capacity of Slovak industry to undertake the massive restructuring that it still needs to undertake if it is to graduate to a product mix less reliant on low wages and cheap access to raw materials.

Conclusions on industrial competitiveness

The integration of Slovak industry into the European market could face difficulties to proceed satisfactorily over the medium term. This will require diversification away from heavy industries and more effective restructuring of enterprises. A major potential impediment to restructuring and diversification efforts is the lack of investment capital due to the low levels of foreign investment, the bad debt

situation and the insider oriented non transparent way of privatization.

Rather than strictly sectoral issues it will be the overall environment in which the Slovak industry is operating, such as infrastructure, taxation, etc., that will determine its future. Thus, the industry will be affected by the economic measures introduced in spring 1997 including the import deposit scheme, and further developments concerning the exchange rate of the Slovak Crown will be of major importance.

An evaluation of the *acquis* specific to the free circulation of industrial goods is to be found in the separate section on the internal market.

Agriculture

The common agricultural policy (CAP) aims to maintain and develop a modern agricultural system ensuring a fair standard of living for the agricultural community and the supply of goods at a reasonable price for consumers, and ensuring the free movement of goods within the EC. Special attention is given to the environment and rural development. Common market organizations exist to administer the CAP. These are complemented by regulations on veterinary health, plant health and animal nutrition and by regulations concerning food hygiene. Legislation also exists in the area of structural policy, originally developed primarily to modernize and enlarge agriculture, but more recently with an increasing emphasis on the environment, and the regional differentiation of the policy. Since reforms in 1992, increasing contributions to farm support have come from direct aid payments compensating cuts in supports prices.

The Europe Agreement with the Slovak Republic provides for preferential trade in the field of agriculture (Articles 19 to 22 with their annexes). Article 78 of the Europe Agreement establishes economic cooperation between the parties to assist in the modernization of agriculture and the agro-industrial sector. The White Paper covers the fields of veterinary, plant health and animal nutrition controls, as well as marketing requirements for individual commodities. The purpose of such legislation is to protect consumers, public health and the health of animals and plants.

Descriptive summary

Agricultural situation

The value of the agricultural production in 1995 was approximately 0.68% of that of the Union.

The share of agriculture in GDP declined from 9.4% in 1989 to 5.8% in 1996. In 1996 employment in agriculture was down to 7.5% of total employment from 12.5% in 1989. The number of employees per 100 ha farm land dropped from 13.3 in 1989 to 6.8 in 1996.

Of the total area of 4.9 million ha, half is used for agricultural purposes and over 40% is covered with forests. About 60% of arable land is planted with cereals, mainly wheat, barley and maize, and about 25% with fodder crops. The other arable crops – oilseeds (mainly rape and sunflower), pulses, sugarbeet and potatoes – are of lesser importance in terms of land use.

Following the transformation and privatization process, basically three forms of farms emerged:

(I) about 1 000 transformed cooperatives managing 69% of agricultural land, with an average size of 1 600 ha;

(II) individual (family) farms: at the end of 1994, there were about 7 600 individual farms (with an average size of 15 ha), most of them created by persons who decided to leave the cooperatives. However, many individual farmers are part-time farmers and more than 60% of the individual farms have less than 5 ha with that area itself having small plots whose average size is 0.34 ha.

(III) There were around 60 corporate farms (joint stock or limited liability) with an average size of 290 ha. Together with the individual (family) farms, these occupied about 9% of the agricultural area in 1994. Owners are usually entrepreneurs organizing land, capital and labour. They are mostly active in the cereals sector.

A further 22% of farmland remains in State farms (137 in 1995), which have an average size of 2 950 hectares. The process of privatization of the State farms has slowed as a result of legislative changes in the scope and methods of privatization.

In 1995, Slovakia was more or less self-sufficient for the main agricultural products (cereals: 3.5 million tonnes; 94.7%; oilseeds: 0.23 million tonnes, 169%, sugarbeet: 1.23 million tonnes, 100%, potatoes: 0.44 million tonnes, 82%; beef: 60 000 tonnes, 94%; pigmeat: 190 000 tonnes, 100%; poultrymeat: 113%; milk 1.19 million tonnes, 130%).

As regards the food industry, 171 enterprises had been privatized by the end of 1996, representing 92% of the total State-owned processing enterprises.

The country is a net importer of agricultural and food products: (export: ECU 430 million; import: ECU 590 million) it accounted for 8% of Slovakia's total imports and 6.2% of its total exports in 1995. Most important agro-food market in terms of value for Slovak exports is the Czech Republic (43% share in 1995), followed by the EU (17%) and the former Soviet Union (15%). On the import side, the Czech Republic is also the most important trade partner (36% share in 1994) followed by the EU (35%). The overall deficit in agro-food foreign trade in 1996 increased by ECU 145 million to ECU 330 million.

In 1995, main Slovak exports were cereals, malt and starch, milk and milk products, vegetables and beverages. The main categories of agro-food imports were tropical products, animal feed, beverages and tobacco.

Agricultural policy

The PSE (producer subsidy equivalent) calculated by the OECD in 1995 was 25% compared to 49% in the EC.

The agricultural market price support is provided mainly by intervention purchases, combined with quotas and export subsidies. The Ministry of Agriculture sets minimum guaranteed prices (covering at least 90% of average production costs and adjusted in case input prices rise by more than 5%) for cereals, slaughter cattle and pigs. In the case of milk, a fixed guaranteed price is set and the policy instruments include a milk quota system, fixed at regional level and distributed to individual farms. Because of shortages on the domestic market, a temporary maximum price has been fixed for potatoes.

The State Fund for Market Regulation (SFMR) makes intervention purchases at the guaranteed price level, provides export subsidies, and grants exports/imports licenses.

In main sectors, an indirect support regime by the Ministry of Agriculture is applied, mainly through input subsidies for purchases of seeds, fertilizers, modern technological equipment, breeding new varieties, irrigation, etc. Exports subsidies are foreseen by the legislation for a number of products including cereals, sugar, beef, pork, poultrymeat, dairy products, fruit and vegetables.

The rural area plays an important role in the socio-economic development of Slovakia and the Slovak Government aims at a gradual adoption of a rural and regional development policy to achieve compatibility with the EU. At present, however, there is no rural development policy similar to EC policies. Direct income support is paid to farmers in less favoured areas in the term of hectare payments varying according to the quality of the soil. Subsidies are also paid (premium per head) for sheep and goat rearing in these regions. Furthermore, subsidies are available for the purchase of high quality inputs (certified seeds, breeding animals) and investments as mentioned above.

Slovak support prices are significantly lower than EC intervention prices. In 1995 the price of cereals was in the range of 56 to 64% of the average European level, and the milk support price was fixed at 63% of the EU price. However, they apply at the farm gate level.

In 1995, the total agricultural budget expenditure amounted to SKK 7 674 million (ECU 200 million), out of which 53% was spent on direct payments to less favoured areas and milk quality payments. Input subsidies accounted for 18% of the agricultural budget while market regulations including export subsidies accounted for 8.5%. General services (training) represented 3% of the total agricultural budget and other support (certain tax reliefs) 9%. In 1995 the absolute amount of support payment represented about 16% of the value of the agricultural production (SKK 48 billion).

In 1993, the taxation system was reformed and several new tax laws were introduced to meet the specific characteristics of the agricultural sector and the goal of adjusting to the EU system. A wide range of tax reliefs and preferences were granted to agriculture.

With the implementation of the Uruguay Round Agreement the variable levies, as well as non-tariffs barriers (compensation levies), were transformed into fixed tariffs. Slovakia has assumed Uruguay Round commitments on domestic support, market access and export subsidies. (SKK 1 651 million, that is ECU 38 million by the year 2000).

In regard to the preferential trade provisions of the Europe Agreement, some quotas have not been filled, mainly because of insufficient marketing and promotion, but also due to the insufficient supply of some of these products.

The Slovak Republic is also a member of CEFTA (Central Europe Free Trade Agreement) which aims at the further liberalization of agricultural trade. Given the fact that other partners in CEFTA have their GATT commitments bound to a higher level of protection than Slovakia, liberalization results in a favourable outcome for Slovakia's exports of agriculture products.

Slovakia is introducing the legislation identified in the White Paper.

Slovakia has an institutional infrastructure with, as the central body for national administration for agriculture, the Ministry of Agriculture; 36 regional land and information services represent the national administration in the districts; in addition, a certain number of 'funds' manage different aspects of agricultural policies. The Slovak Agricultural and Food Chamber (SKPPK), which is a non-State, public and autonomous institution, cooperates with the Ministry in establishing the agrarian policy.

Current and prospective assessment

After a five-year gap in investment, there is an important need for the replacement of machinery. In the medium term Slovakia is expected to produce increasing exportable surpluses of cereals, oil seed, sugar, pigmeat and poultry.

Even though Slovakia has made progress in adopting new legislation and structures compatible with the EU, major differences remain between the Slovak and EU policies related to agriculture.

In implementing its agricultural policy programme of 1993, the Slovak Government has been quite successful in fulfilling its objectives of ensuring economic stability and supporting agriculture. The revision of the current policy programme foreseen in 1998 is not expected to fundamentally change the current policy framework.

Adjustments of certain market organizations are necessary, however, in order to bring the sector more closely in line with that in the EU. Import and export arrangements will have to be adapted to match the Union's. Import and export licences currently applied would have to be abandoned. Also certain input subsidies (for ex-purchase of fertilizers, breeding of new varieties) are granted which appear to be inconsistent with the *acquis*.

The main market policy instruments applied in the EC are not applied in Slovakia. These include key instruments like sugar quotas, main arable crop schemes (base area, compensatory payment scheme), as well as certain rural and structural development programmes.

Management and control of these schemes will require relatively sophisticated administrative systems, including an appropriate land register and cattle identification and registration systems. The Slovak administrative capacity would need to be further developed in these areas if these measures were to be applied in Slovakia. Producers' organizations and wholesale markets in the fruit and vegetable sector need to be set up.

It is difficult to foresee the development of agricultural support prices in Slovakia in the period before accession. This will depend on a number of factors including the domestic economy, the situation on export markets and the development of price support levels in the Union.

In general, the food processing industry is still suffering from over-capacity and is in need of modernization.

As far as rural policy is concerned, at present, there is insufficient coordination of financial support for rural development programmes between the various sectoral bodies at horizontal and regional level. Horizontal and regional measures often overlap. Responsibility for rural development policy at national level has not been clearly assigned.

Negotiations are ongoing to solve the difficulties which have arisen in the application of the trade provisions of the Europe Agreement.

The Slovak Republic is making progress in introducing the legislation identified in the White Paper. In the veterinary and phytosanitary field, Slovakia is negotiating an agreement on equivalency with the European Commission. The negotiations are nearing completion.

For the wine sector, current rules of classification of individual wine varieties and their cultivation are based on an Act of 1964. An Act on Viticulture approximated to EC legislation has been adopted. It will require changes in the structure and the system of registration, filing and control. It will also necessitate the reinforcement of inspection bodies in terms of staff and equipment. Slovakia is an OIV member (Organisation internationale de la vigne et du vin).

As far as marketing requirements are concerned, a revised Food Codex is planned to enter into force during 1997. Slovak technical standards will have to be adapted and should also cover phytosanitary aspects.

In the fruit and vegetables sector, it seems there is no inspection at entry to Slovakia (frontiers, ports, airports), as required in the EC legislation. Inspection bodies at the frontier points would have to be created.

In the veterinary field approximation to, and an implementation of, the *acquis* has been partly achieved. Further progress is needed in the adoption and implementation of the new veterinary and breeding basic legislation.

The timetables for the approval and implementation of secondary legislation in the different sections vary from 1997 until the year 2000.

Traditionally the Slovak Republic had a well-established infrastructure for veterinary control and inspection, both at the borders and internally, under the Ministry of Agriculture.

Due to some administrative changes in the veterinary structure at the regional level, some difficulties may be expected in implementation and enforcement of new legislation. In the approximation process, further adaptation will be needed with regard to the concept of HACCP (hazard analysis critical control point) and auto-control, monitoring and surveillance programmes, disease eradication (in particular classical swine fever), internal market control measures (safeguard, the license system, veterinary checks, additional guarantees, regionalization), import regime (approved third countries, approved establishments) and the identification and registration system of animals (particularly back yard holdings). The facilities and professional experience at border inspection posts and veterinary laboratories need upgrading. The computerized information system, the identification and registration system of animals, and the rendering infrastructure need to be improved. In general, the implementation of the *acquis* should be achievable to a large extent on the medium term.

As regards seeds and propagation material, and plant health, harmonization with EC legislation is well advanced, and new laws are in preparation. The structures to adequately implement the legislation need to be strengthened.

Progress is being made in the approximation of animal nutrition, plant protection products and pesticide residues legislation. Further exchange of information between the Commission and the Slovakian authorities will be needed generally and in relation to the structure for implementation.

Conclusion

Further alignment to the Community *acquis* is still necessary although significant progress has been made in adopting the measures mentioned in the White Paper.

Particular efforts are needed in relation to:

☐ implementation and enforcement of veterinary and phytosanitary requirements and upgrading of establishments to meet EC standards; this is particularly important with regard to the inspection and control arrangements for protecting the EU external border;

☐ strengthening of the administrative structures to ensure the necessary capacity to implement and enforce the instruments of the CAP;

☐ further substantial restructuring of the agro-food sector to improve its competitive capacity.

If such progress is accomplished, accession in the medium term should not be accompanied by significant problems in applying the common agricultural policy in an appropriate manner.

Fisheries

The common fisheries policy includes common market organizations, structural policy, agreements with third countries, management and conservation of fish resources, and scientific research in support of these activities.

The Europe Agreement includes provisions concerning trade in fisheries products with the Community. The White Paper includes no measures in this field.

Descriptive summary

Slovakia has only inland water fisheries and the sector is not very important to its economy. In 1995 the production was 6 015 tonnes. There are only 25 State and private producers.

As a trading partner of the Community, Slovakia represents 0.01% of EC total imports (independently of origin) of fisheries products and 0.40% of EC imports of fisheries products from the candidate countries alone (in terms of value). As regards EC exports, Slovakia receives 0.32% of our total exports of fisheries products and 3.8% of our exports of these products to the candidate countries (in terms of value).

Current and prospective assessment

Slovakia's production and foreign trade data, when compared to the corresponding EC figures, are quite low and therefore should not have a significant impact upon the Community as a whole. It will be necessary for Slovakia to ensure compliance with the EC's health, hygiene and environmental standards.

Conclusion

The fisheries sector does not present a problem for accession.

Energy

Main EU energy policy objectives, as reflected in the Commission White Paper 'An energy policy for the EU' include enhancement of competitiveness, security of energy supplies and protection of the environment. Key elements of the energy *acquis* comprise Treaty provisions and secondary legislation particularly concerning competition and State aids, internal energy market (including directives on electricity, price transparency, gas and electricity transit, hydrocarbons licensing, emergency response including security stock obligations, etc.), nuclear energy, as well as energy efficiency and environmental rules. Development of trans-European energy networks and support for energy R&D are other important elements of energy policy. Ongoing developments include liberalization of the gas sector, energy efficiency *acquis* and the auto-oil programme.

In the field of nuclear energy, the Community *acquis* has evolved substantially from the original EAEC Treaty to a framework of legal and political instruments, including international agreements. At present, it addresses issues of health and safety, including radiation protection, safety of nuclear installations, management of radioactive waste, investment including EURATOM financial instruments, promotion of research, nuclear common market, supplies, safeguards, and international relations.

The Europe Agreement provides for cooperation to develop the progressive integration of the energy markets in Europe and includes provisions on assistance within the related policy areas. The White Paper preparing CEECs for the internal energy market underlines the need for full application of key internal market directives in combination with EC competition law. As to the nuclear sector, the White Paper refers to nuclear supply safeguards and shipments of nuclear waste.

Descriptive summary

Slovakia is heavily dependent on external energy resources, importing more than 80% of its needs, particularly oil, gas and nuclear fuel from Russia.

The limited indigenous resources (poor quality lignite and brown coal) present severe environmental consequences and are mined with State interventions. It is intended to continue current production levels (3.7 million tonnes) until at least 2005.

The Slovak energy sector is two to three times less efficient than the EU-average, due to past supply oriented policies, low prices and the heavy industry structure.

Slovakia is a strategic transit country, both for the EU and the region, for Russian gas, and transit and storage capacities are being enlarged. Its electricity networks have been, since October 1995, synchronously linked as a test to the western European UCPTE network.

Slovakia operates, at Jaslovské Bohunice, two VVER 440-230 (first generation) and two VVER 440-213 (second generation) nuclear reactors representing nearly half of the electricity production. For Units 1 and 2, after a short-term improvement programme, they are currently further upgraded (1996-1999) and should then increase the safety level towards EC safety standards. Finally, the early A1 prototype reactor had to be shut down prematurely in 1977 and is currently being decommissioned. Its spent fuel is being shipped to Russia. At Mochovce, two VVER 440-213 reactors are under construction with some participation of western firms and they should be on stream within the next two years. Two more units of the same type are foreseen on the site for the first decade of the next century. The safety of this nuclear power plant will be considered to be close to safety objectives generally accepted in the EU, once the upgrading programme is completed. There is no uranium mining or nuclear fuel fabrication.

Current and prospective assessment

Slovakia's energy policy objectives are in line with those of the EU and include introduction of more competition; enhanced security of supply, environmental protection and energy efficiency.

The competition framework in the energy sector does not yet fulfil the directives of the internal energy market in combination with the application of EC competition law. The application of the 1994 Slovak anti-monopoly law does not offer sufficient guarantees for competition in the sector according to EC *acquis*, although there has been progress in creating conditions for the unbundling of accounts of the generation and transmission part of the electricity company. It is therefore necessary to speed up the adoption and future implementation of the Energy Act.

The sector is characterized by State-dominated monopolies, although a measure of liberalization and privatization is ongoing in the oil and coal sector. Act 192/95 excludes, for strategic reasons, certain activities in the electricity and gas sector as well as in oil pipeline transport from privatization.

Energy prices, particularly gas, electricity and heat prices for households are cross-subsidised and do not cover costs. The government is expected to decide shortly on a policy to phase these distortions out by the year 2002.

Slovakia has started developing legislation on emergency preparedness, including building up oil stocks. At present, the country does not meet the 90 days of stock requirement for emergency oil stocks (stocks are estimated at 40 to 45 days of consumption) and cannot, due to the needed investments, be realistically expected to reach this target in the short term.

Restructuring of the mining sector is unavoidable and its social and regional consequences will have to be addressed, whereas State interventions should be assessed against EC State aid rules.

Slovakia has started the development of EC conform efficiency legislation (e.g. labelling appliances, minimum efficiency norms) as well as environmental norms (e.g. fuel quality standards), but more remains to be done. The adoption of an Energy Saving Law will underpin future compliance with efficiency *acquis*. It should be noted that the upgrading of the national refinery to meet EC standards will require considerable investments and that the refinery will have to compete on a saturated European market.

A government resolution proposed nuclear fuel supply diversification from 1999 onwards. Accession by the Slovak Republic would increase the EU's dependence on Russian uranium and enrichment. But the plan to diversify its supply sources in the future would be in line with the common nuclear materials supply policy of security through diversification of sources which would apply to supply contracts concluded after accession.

Spent fuel from Bohunice was shipped back to the Soviet Union until 1986 but has since been stored in pools at the site. All spent fuel from the A1 reactor will be returned to Russia by 1999 in the frame of a former Czechoslovakia/Soviet Union agreement. An increase in the storage capacity of the existing pools is under study. Longer term intermediate storage and final disposal options of spent fuel are also being studied. Low level and medium level waste repository is under licensing at Mochovce.

Upon accession, the Slovak Republic will need to comply with the provisions of the Euratom Treaty, in particular those related to supply of nuclear material, the nuclear common market, safeguards, health and safety and international agreements. It is party to all relevant international regimes and conventions. The Slovak Republic also has a full-scope safeguards agreement with the IAEA, and in this and the other areas above, no major difficulties in applying Community legislation are expected. Nevertheless, the problem of nuclear safety has to be dealt with and realistic programmes, including effective closure when necessary, have to be agreed upon and implemented. The independence of the safety authority should be supported.

Conclusion

Slovakia needs to step up its efforts in order to comply with most of the EC energy legislation in the next few years. In particular, matters such as the adjustment of monopolies including import and export issues, access to networks, energy pricing, emergency preparedness including the building up of mandatory oil stocks, State interventions in the solid fuels sector, and the development of energy efficiency and fuel quality standards need to be closely followed.

No major difficulties are foreseen for compliance with Euratom provisions. Nuclear safety requires continued particular attention. Safety standards should be tackled appropriately and realistic programmes implemented quickly. Longer term solutions for waste need attention.

Transport

Community transport policy consist of policies and initiatives in three fundamental areas:

☐ Improving quality by developing integrated and competitive transport systems based on advanced technologies which also contribute to environmental and safety objectives.

☐ Improving the functioning of the single market in order to promote efficiency, choice and user-friendly provision of transport services while safeguarding social standards;

☐ Broadening the external dimension by improving transport links with third countries and fostering the access of EU operators to other transport markets (the common transport policy action programme, 1995-2000).

The Europe Agreement provides for approximation of legislation with Community law and cooperation aiming to restructure and modernize transport, the improvement of access to the transport market, the facilitation of transit and the achievement of operating standards comparable to those in the Community. The White Paper focuses on measures for the accomplishment of internal market conditions in the transport sector, including such aspects as competition, legislative harmonization and standards.

Descriptive summary

The Slovak transport infrastructure has a strong East-West orientation, largely due to the particular topography of the country, but also related to close linkages with the Czech Republic, built up during the time of the former Czechoslovakia. The mountains in north-central Slovakia divide the country into two dominant economic areas (Bratislava in west Slovakia and Kosice in the east) and form a natural barrier to north-south transport. This has significant implications on the comparative cost of infrastructures. Border crossings with neighbouring countries are few and require extensive modernization. The Slovak Government adopted an ambitious plan of motorway construction in February 1996 in order to accelerate the integration of Slovakia into the trans-European multimodal transport corridors. The Slovakian territory is crossed by three of these corridors.

There has been a significant move away from rail and inland waterways to public road passenger transport, despite a rapid growth in car ownership and use. For the moment, however, the railways remain the most important means of transport.

Current and prospective assessment

In terms of the internal market, the Slovak Republic is relatively well advanced in adapting its legislation to the Community acquis. The international transport sector in Slovakia to a large extent already applies rules similar to those applied in the Community, particularly to maritime transport, inland waterways and combined transport. New legislation on civil aviation, largely in line with Community rules, is in preparation. However, particular attention will have to be paid to improving safety standards. In the railway sector, the amendments made to Slovak legislation to ensure compliance with Community rules on access to the rail network and the separation of accounts for the management and the use of infrastructures and the real application of legislation on public service provision and the standardization of accounts will have to be monitored over the coming years. Legislation on international road haulage complies with most of the Community rules but operation of the domestic road haulage sector poses more of a problem. This will have to be monitored and is particularly important in the context of a future Union without internal borders where cabotage in road haulage will be totally liberalized. There are also problems with market access, safety inspection, technical standards and taxation.

Road passenger transport appears to comply with Community legislation, but its current structure, which dates from 1989 and only includes State enterprises, could cause problems in future.

The development of an integrated and competitive transport system is a goal accepted by the Slovak authorities. The main difficulties are likely to be in achieving satisfactory levels of safety, and efficient use of the transport system. Slovakia has made relatively satisfactory progress on safety. However, achieving a coherent transport system appears to be more difficult. The share taken by road transport is likely to continue to grow and Slovakia will have to concentrate its efforts on promoting use of the rail network and inland waterways, which it is already attempting to do.

As regards improving links with the Member States of the Community and with its neighbours, Slovakia has not so far drawn on international financing to develop its infrastructures. It is, however, planning to invest ECU 2 billion from the national budget between 1995 and 1999 in transport infrastructures used by international traffic, particularly the pan-European corridors. This is around 2.8% of GNP, which would appear satisfactory, but any reduction of this amount owing to budgetary constraints could pose problems.

Conclusion

The Slovak Republic has made progress in adapting transport legislation to the *acquis*. Considerable progress still needs to be made, however, on road haulage (particularly market access, safety standards and taxation) and railways, where the effective adaptation of legislation will have to be monitored. The situation in these two sectors must improve if the transport sector is not to pose serious difficulties as regards the adoption of the internal market *acquis*.

Steps must also be taken to ensure that the means required to lay the basis for the extension to the accession countries of the trans-European transport network are provided. This requires particular attention because Slovakia, as a mountainous country, faces higher costs in constructing infrastructures, which places the country at a disadvantage compared with neighbouring countries in which TENs are being more easily developed. Finally, Slovak administrative structures, including inspection bodies, for example those in the area of safety, should be rapidly and significantly strengthened at all levels to prevent them further slowing the country's progress.

Small and medium enterprises

EU enterprise policy aims at encouraging a favourable environment for the development of SMEs throughout the EU, at improving their competitiveness and encouraging their Europeanization and internationalization. It is characterized by a high degree of subsidiarity. The complementary role of the Community is defined and implemented through a multiannual programme for SMEs in the EU. This programme provides the legal and budgetary basis for the Community's specific SME policy actions. The *acquis* has so far been limited to recommendations on specific areas, although legislation in other sectors also affects SMEs (e.g. competition, environment, company law).

The Europe Agreement provides for cooperation to develop and strengthen SMEs, in particular in the private sector, *inter alia* through provision of information and assistance on legal, administrative and tax conditions. The White Paper contains no specific measures.

Descriptive summary

Since 1989 the increase in the number and importance of SMEs has been impressive. The number of SMEs has grown to 300 000 in 1995 and they now account for 35% of gross output in the industrial sector. In some sectors such as construction, road transportation, and distribution this contribution is much higher (approximately 80%). In terms of employment, there are 425 000 SME employees and the combined share of SMEs represents roughly 25% of total employment. Slovakia, with 54 enterprises per 1 000 inhabitants, is above the EU average of 41. Comparative studies show that Slovakia has experienced the most dynamic growth of SMEs in the region.

Much of this growth has been spurred on by the privatization process in which 10 000 companies were auctioned off in 1992-93. Most of these SMEs were craftsmen and tradesmen rather than legal entities. Very small enterprises of self-employed people represent more than 80% of the SME sector. The post-privatization growth also results from 'spin-offs' as many large companies rationalize. SME growth has been particularly noticeable in the machinery, fabricated metal product and textile sectors.

The basic legal framework pertaining to entrepreneurial activity in general is applicable to SMEs. In addition the Slovak Government adopted a specific law on SME support in 1995. The primary forms of support are loans, loan guarantees, reimbursement of interest, contributions according to the specific regulations, refundable financial assistance and subsidies. Cooperatives are also regulated in the

Commercial Code while mutualities and foundations are regulated in the Civil Code. In 1993 an amendment to the tax law was passed allowing tax breaks for certain newly established companies.

SME development as a government priority is defined in the government's industrial policy. The National Agency for Support to SMEs (NADSME) was established in August 1993 to encourage the development and growth of SMEs and coordinate all support activities (advisory and financial) to SMEs. There are also 12 regional advisory and information centres (RAICs) whose role is to provide advisory and information services as well as several other support structures such as business innovation centres and various NGOs.

Current and prospective assessment

Significant progress has been made in the development of the SME sector and Slovakia has shown a strong commitment to developing and strengthening SMEs and EU-Slovak cooperation in the field as foreseen under Article 90 of the Europe Agreement. The conditions for sustainable SME growth and development are basically in place. There is, however, further room for improvement. There is a need for simplification of legislation to make it more SME friendly, strengthening of the support infrastructure, improvement of the tax environment and the development of the SMEs access to financing and their ability to penetrate new markets.

Buoyancy in the SME sector may be constrained over the medium term by a lack of access to needed investment capital.

The on-going efforts to strengthen the SMEs during the pre-accession period will therefore need to be continued.

Conclusion

There are no specific problems foreseen in Slovakia's integration in this sector.

3.5. Economic and social cohesion

Employment and social affairs

Community social policy has been developed through a variety of instruments such as legal provisions, the European Social Fund and actions focused on specific issues, including public health, poverty and the disabled. The legal acquis covers health and safety at work, labour law and working conditions, equal opportunities for men and women, social security coordination for migrant workers and tobacco products. Social legislation in the Union has been characterized by laying down minimum standards. In addition, the social dialogue at European level is enshrined in the Treaty (Article 118B), and the Protocol on social policy refers to consultation of the social partners and measures to facilitate the social dialogue.

The Europe Agreement provides for approximation of legislation with Community law and cooperation on improving standards of health and safety at work, labour market policies and the modernization of the social security system. It also provides for Community workers legally employed in Slovakia to be treated without discrimination on grounds of nationality as regards their working conditions. The White Paper provides for measures for approximation in all the areas of the *acquis*.

Descriptive summary

In the Slovak Republic the reform of the social dialogue which was initiated in the former Czechoslovakia has slowed down since 1993. An important element in further reform will be the government's development of respect for the autonomous character of the social partners in the framework of political life. The most representative organization on the employer's side, the Slovak Association of Employer's Unions is a member of the Union of Industrial and Employers' Confederation of Europe (UNICE) and of the International Organization of Employers. The Slovak Confederation of Trade Unions, which is the most representative organization, is a member of the European Trade Union Confederation (ETUC).

Over recent years registered unemployment has been hovering at a relatively high level. In 1996, it was at 10.9% according to ILO methodology. Regional differences in employment rates are considerable, with unemployment being particularly high in the south and south-eastern regions of the country. The number of long-term unemployed has increased significantly and youth unemployment is high and shows no sign of decline.

A network of regional and local employment offices has been established to implement labour market policies. The Slovak Republic has introduced measures to make the labour market more flexible and a continuation of this process will be needed for integration into the EU labour market and employment policies.

Social security in the Slovak Republic aims at establishing a threefold system composed of social insurance, State social support and social assistance. Since the introduction of the unemployment benefits system in 1991, the rate of registered unemployment has increased quite significantly, but the beneficiary ratio has dropped sharply. The collection system gives rise to significant administration problems, including difficulties of collecting contributions from employers and the self-employed. In many cases, there is a lack of information about the availability of benefits and the conditions of eligibility. Social expenditure accounts for about 30% of total government expenditure and for approximately 14% of GDP. Pensions are the largest expenditure item. Continued efforts are required to ensure that measures of social protection are developed.

The Slovak health system needs to be significantly improved.

Current and prospective assessment

Health and safety legislation in the Slovak Republic is in the process of being modified in terms of both orientations and specific provisions. New proposals taking account of EU directives on health and safety at work are being drafted. Additional legislative initiatives will be needed to ensure full compliance with the *acquis*. The Slovak inspection structures are not in accordance with the ILO Convention No. 81, but Slovakia intends to establish independent inspection structures with appropriate control methods to comply with ILO rules.

Slovakia is relatively advanced in the area of labour law on issues such as protection against collective dismissal, maximum working time and adequate rest periods, minimum paid annual leave and the right to collective bargaining. Various amendments, however, are required to ensure full compliance with EC rules on the protection of workers in the event of insolvency of their employer. The existing rules of information and consultation of workers as requested by a number of EU directives should be further developed. Slovakia is planning a new Labour Code in order to ensure compatibility with EU requirements.

On equal opportunity, the basic provisions of EC non-discrimination law between women and men are covered by Slovak legislation.

Concerning the right to the free movement of workers, there would appear to be no obstacles to prevent Slovakia from being able to implement the provisions of the *acquis* in this area. The introduction of the right to free movement will, however, require changes in national law, particularly as regards access to employment and a treatment free from discrimination on grounds of nationality.

In the field of social security for migrant workers accession does not, in principle, pose major problems, although some technical adaptations will be necessary. More important is the administrative capacity to apply the detailed coordination rules in cooperation with other countries. The Slovak Republic is developing some of the administrative structures required to carry out these tasks, but further preparation and training will be necessary before the coordination rules can be applied.

Concerning the two EC directives covering tobacco issues, Slovakia has recently agreed a law which would satisfy EU requirements concerning the warning labelling of cigarette packages. There is apparently no legislation matching the second tobacco directive imposing a maximum tar content on cigarettes.

Conclusion

Since 1993, the Slovak Republic has taken a number of significant steps in preparation for its future EU-membership. But social reforms need to be further developed, the social dialogue needs to be ameliorated and the health system to be improved. Slovakia needs to make substantive progress in the fields of health and safety at work and labour law to ensure realignment with EU standards. Efforts to implement the *acquis* effectively need to be continued. If the Slovak Republic pursues its important efforts, both in terms of adoption and of application of the EC acquis it should be possible to take on the obligations of EU membership in the medium term.

Regional policy and cohesion

In accordance with Title XIV of the Treaty, the Community supports the strengthening of cohesion, mainly through the Structural Funds. Slovakia will have to implement these instruments effectively whilst respecting the principles, objectives and procedures which will be in place at the time of its accession.

The Europe Agreement provides for cooperation on regional development and spatial planning, notably through the exchange of information between local, regional and national authorities and the exchange of civil servants and experts. The White Paper contains no specific provisions.

Descriptive summary

In 1995, Slovakia's GDP/per capita stood at some 41% of the EU average. There are marked regional disparities in Slovakia. Out of the 38 districts which existed prior to the creation of a new regional administrative structure in July 1996, over 50% of GDP was created in the four districts of Bratislava, Kosice, Trnava and Banka Bystrica, with Bratislava alone contributing 32% of Slovakia's total GDP. These four districts received over 62% of total investment in Slovakia.

Likewise, in looking at unemployment figures, districts where unemployment has stabilized or is decreasing are in the main urban areas (Bratislava and Kosice) and in the heavily industrialized area close to the Czech border in the north-west. The regions with the highest incidence of unemployment are located in the southern and eastern parts of the country. By way of illustration, while Bratislava registers 4.6% unemployment, the corresponding figure for the worst hit district (Rimaska Sobota) in the south-east is 26%.

With a view to creating a regional level of administration, a law was passed in July 1996 on 'Territorial and administrative arrangement of the Slovak Republic' which has established 8 regions and 79 districts. A second law was passed at the same time relating to the new organization of local State administrations, following the modifications in the regional structure.

Hitherto, the Slovak Republic has implemented its regional development initiatives through sectoral policies on the basis of the 'principles for economic policy'. Indeed, a legal basis for regional development policy does not exist at the present stage.

Nevertheless, a draft Act on Regional Development is currently being elaborated which would constitute a new legal framework for a prospective regional policy.

The institutional structure of Slovakia's regional polica is characterized by the predominant position of government. Indeed, regional development initiatives are subject to a final decision by the government. The Office for the Strategy of Developing the Society, Science and Technology (OSDSST), a State body, ensures the proper implementation of these initiatives and is associated to the drafting. However, it role is foremost consultative. The role of district administration is limited to the implementation of State projects.

The Slovak Republic' financial instruments at the disposal of regional development initiatives are clearly limited. However, the share of development related expenditures which could constitute potential counterpart funds to EC structural policy cannot yet be determined. Therefore, the Slovak Republic's co-financing capacity cannot presently be evaluated with sufficient reliability.

Current and prospective assessment

The Slovak Republic's regional development initiatives are implemented through sectoral policies and coordinated, at central level, by the regional policy guarantor (OSDSST). The financial resources at the disposal of Slovakia's regional policy instruments are limited.

In addition, the operational and organizational framework of Slovakia's regional policy suffers from some serious deficiencies. Regional policy decision-making is overly centralized with all major decisions taken directly by the government. A more distinct ministerial responsibility is necessary and inter-ministerial coordination is to be improved in order to increase the efficiency of the decision-making process within the field of regional policy. Special attention needs to be focused on strengthening Slovak capacity to programme, manage, evaluate and control Community funding.

Finally, Slovakia is clearly in need of an adequate legal basis determining the principles, objectives and mode of operation guiding its regional development initiatives.

Conclusion

The Slovak Republic presents only limited elements of an integrated development policy which could ensure compliance with EC structural policy rules. A comprehensive differentiated policy addressing regional disparities should be introduced. Moreover, the Slovak Republic's administrative capacity to manage integrated regional development programmes clearly needs to be improved. Thus, significant reforms including the establishment of appropriate administrative and budgetary procedures need to be implemented before the Slovak Republic can apply the Community rules and to channel effectively the funds from the EC structural policies.

3.6. Quality of life and environment

Environment

The Community's environmental policy, derived from the Treaty, aims towards sustainability based on the integration of environmental protection into EU sectoral policies, preventive action, the polluter pays principle, fighting environmental damage at the source, and shared responsibility. The *acquis* comprises approximately 200 legal acts covering a wide range of matters, including water and air pollution, management of waste and chemicals, biotechnology, radiation protection, and nature protection. Member States are required to ensure that an environmental impact assessment is carried out before development consent is granted for certain public and private projects.

The Europe Agreement stipulates that Slovak development policies shall be guided by the principle of sustainable development and should fully incorporate environmental considerations. It also identifies environment as a priority for bilateral cooperation, as well as an area for approximation legislation to that of the Community.

The White Paper covers only a small part of the environmental *acquis*, namely product-related legislation, which is directly related to the free circulation of goods.

Descriptive summary

Slovakia's environmental problems remain significant, despite improvement during the last years. The most serious problems are surface and ground water pollution, waste management, and local air quality.

Environmental quality has improved significantly, largely thanks to restructuring of heavy industry. In particular, air pollution from heavy industries has significantly decreased since 1989, and hot-spots are now limited to major industrial areas (Bratislava, Kosice, Banka Bystrica). Important problems exist in the water sector, in particular low connection rate of households to sewage systems and often largely uncontrolled industrial effluent. Improvements have been made in the area of hazardous and municipal waste but problems remain substantial and treatment/storage inadequate. New pollution sources such as traffic and light manufacturing have emerged and need to be addressed. Slovakia possesses areas of great natural value, which would represent an asset to the environment of an enlarged Union

Slovakia has undertaken a comprehensive reform of its environmental legislation. A framework environmental act (1992), a strategy of national environmental policy (1993) and an action programme (1996) have been adopted. Their objectives and principles are adjusted towards sustainable development, prevention, correction at the source, the 'polluter pays' principle, etc. The principle of

integrating environmental issues into other policies is contained in the 1994 act on environmental impact assessment. However, the introduction of integrated pollution prevention and control and further 'framework' type legislation as well as adequate enforcement scheduling regulations is needed. Existing agencies and structures need to be strengthened, their responsibilities clarified and their operations re-orientated to incorporate better the emergent pollution sources. Slovakia's expenditure on environmental investment as a percentage of GDP has been significant in recent years.

Current and prospective assessment

A considerable effort has been made to establish environmental legislation compatible with Community law. On the basis of a strategy for the implementation of the White Paper, progress has been made in adopting a number of White Paper measures such as legislation on the lead content in petrol and on waste management. Alignment in relation to other Stage I measures including radiation protection, chemical substances, control of risks of existing substances, environmental consequences of the deliberate release of genetically modified organisms is foreseen by 2000 at the earliest. Stage II measures are scheduled to be in place two to three years later. Approximation has been taking place in other areas of the environmental acquis as well. The new air quality law, with its redefinition of administrative competencies, has been in place since July 1996. A new water act is being prepared.

Slovakia is in the process of elaborating a detailed environmental accession strategy which should be ready by the end of 1997. Particular attention should be given to the quick transposition of framework directives dealing with air, waste, water, and the integrated pollution prevention and control (IPPC) directive, as well as the establishment of financing strategies for legislation in the water, air and waste sectors requiring major investments.

In the area of effective implementation and enforcement of the EC acquis, problems are considerably greater: substantive compliance with EC standards is low in waste, water (especially in certain industrial areas), and air (for certain regions and municipalities). Polluters are not being effectively monitored and/or prosecuted. Inconsistencies in the legislation – especially between framework legislation and secondary legislation on implementation – hamper effective pollution monitoring and enforcement. While the monitoring system is basically sound, processing of data is a problem which needs to be addressed. The country's environmental accession strategy should include implementation timetables for meeting the EU environmental *acquis*, starting amongst others with implementation of the framework and IPPC directives mentioned above.

Key problems which currently hinder effective compliance include inadequate enforcement of standards; insufficient financial resources, especially at the municipal level; weak administrative structures and lack of clarity on division of responsibilities among agencies and levels of government; and inadequate public awareness and participation.

Conclusion

If Slovakia perseveres in its present legislative programme, full transposition of the *acquis* should be achieved in the medium term. On the other hand, effective compliance with a number of pieces of legislation requiring a sustained high level of investment and considerable administrative effort (e.g. urban waste water treatment,drinking water, aspects of waste management and air pollution legislation) could be achieved only in the long to very long term.

Consumer protection

The Community *acquis* covers protection of economic interests of consumers (including control of misleading advertising, indication of prices, consumer credit, unfair contract terms, distance selling, package travel, sales away from business premises and timeshare property) as well as general safety of goods and the specific sectors of cosmetics, textile names and toys.

The Europe Agreement provides for approximation of legislation with Community law and cooperation with a view to achieving full compatibility between the systems of consumer protection in Slovakia and the Community. Stage I measures of the White Paper focus on improving product safety, including cosmetics, textiles and toys, and on the protection of the economic interests of the consumer, notably measures on misleading advertising, consumer credit, unfair contract terms and indication of prices. Stage II measures relate to package travel, sales away from business premises and time-share property. New EC legislation which has been adopted recently (distance selling) or will be adopted soon (comparative advertising, price indication) will also need to be taken into account.

Descriptive summary

Slovak consumer protection legislation consists of a general consumer protection law passed in 1992 which regulates the responsibilities of the public administration in the field of consumer protection and sets out the rights of consumers and consumer protection associations. The Ministry of Economy is responsible for consumer protection and policy while the Trade Inspection within the Ministry is entitled to implement and enforce the Consumer Protection Act in cooperation with other testing and inspection authorities. The Consumer Policy Council acts as an advisory body to the Minister of Economy on consumer policy and priorities and has representatives from all relevant State authorities, consumer associations, trade and industry. Consumer organizations have a legal right to work with public authorities in both developing and monitoring consumer policy as well as in improving the effectiveness of its administration.

Current and prospective assessment

At the institutional level, the Slovak Republic appears well placed to continue the process of implementation of EC and international consumer protection norms. Relations between the non-governmental organizations and the administration appear to be constructive. The Slovak Consumer Protection Act is more general and less complete than the detailed provisions of EC directives on consumer protection as set out in the White Paper. Full compatibility with EC directives has almost been reached on general product safety, and partial compliance has been attained regarding indication of prices. A new Advertising Act adopted in 1996 brings this field of consumer law closer to EC provisions.

In various areas, the rules applicable to consumer safety ensure a better level of protection to consumers than is the case under the European directive. Separate draft decrees on the safety of toys and on textile names are under preparation, and legislation on consumer credit and amendments to the Act on Consumer Protection is being drafted. Full compliance with White Paper measures is foreseen by the Slovak authorities by the year 2000.

The development of a strong and independent consumer movement, sustained by public authorities, will need to accompany the introduction of the *acquis*.

Conclusion

Although Slovakia will need to make efforts to complete the legislative programme in line with EC requirements and to strengthen the administration as well as consumer organizations, Slovakia is likely be in a position to take on the acquis on consumer protection in the medium term.

3.7. Justice and home affairs

The present provisions

The justice and home affairs (JHA) acquis principally derives from the framework for cooperation set out in Title VI (Article K) of the Treaty on European Union (TEU), 'the third pillar', although certain 'first pillar' (EC Treaty) provisions and legislative measures are also closely linked

The EU JHA framework primarily covers: asylum; control of external borders and immigration; customs cooperation and police cooperation against serious crime, including drug trafficking; and judicial cooperation on criminal and civil matters. The TEU stipulates key principles upon which such cooperation is based, notably the European Convention on Human Rights and the 1951 Geneva Convention on the Status of Refugees. It is also based implicitly on a range of international conventions concerning its fields of interest, notably those of the Council of Europe, the United Nations and the Hague Conference. The legislative content of third pillar *acquis* is different from the first pillar; it consists of conventions, joint actions, joint positions and resolutions, (including the agreed elements of draft instruments which are in negotiation). A number of EU conventions (including the 1990 Dublin Convention, and conventions relating to extradition, fraud and Europol) have been agreed by the Council and are now in the process of ratification by national Parliaments; several other conventions, including one on external frontiers are in various stages of negotiation in the Council. The JHA *acquis* involves a high degree of practical cooperation, as well as legislation and its effective implementation.

The new Treaty

For many of the above matters, the entry into force of the Treaty resulting from the Amsterdam Intergovernmental Conference will mark the end of the current cooperation framework.

Reiterating the objective of developing the Union into an 'area of freedom, security and justice', the new Treaty brings these matters, including the free movement of persons, asylum and immigration, into the Community's sphere of competence.

On the free movement of persons in particular, the new Treaty provides for the incorporation of the Schengen *acquis* into the framework of the European Union and binds any candidate for EU membership to accept that acquis in full.

With regard to matters remaining within the cooperation framework, namely policing and criminal justice, the new Treaty provides for the reinforcement of the cooperation system.

The Europe Agreement and the White Paper

The Europe Agreement includes provision for cooperation in the fight against drug abuse and money laundering.

The White Paper does not deal directly with third pillar subjects, but reference is made to first pillar matters such as money laundering and freedom of movement of persons which are closely related to justice and home affairs considerations. Reference is also made to the Brussels and Rome conventions.

Descriptive summary

General preconditions for JHA cooperation

Slovakia joined the Council of Europe in 1993 and has ratified the most important instruments concerning human rights. The Constitution provides for an independent judiciary according to the rule of law.

Some progress has been made in the reform of JHA institutions. The Constitution guarantees data protection: a new data protection law to be presented during 1997 is expected to cover all EU requirements in this field. Slovakia has not yet signed the 1990 data protection convention. (See also separate section on the single market).

Asylum

Slovakia has acceded to the Geneva Convention. The Constitution provides for asylum and the 1995 Refugee Act is based on EU practice, including provision for accelerated procedures and the 'safe third country' principle. Implementation of the new law is now well under way, but refugees have limited legal back-up and staff in the Migration Office lack knowledge and experience of conditions in third countries. In 1995 300 applications for asylum were made. There are also temporary refugees from former Yugoslavia; the first returns took place in March 1996 in cooperation with the UNHCR/IOM. Some 400 applications for asylum were made in 1996.

Immigration/border control

Some 89 million border crossings were made in 1995; of these some 2 000 were revealed as being illegal. Slovakia is working towards the EU list of third countries for which visas are required, but visa-free agreements are still in place with Belarus, Russia, Cuba, Romania, Bulgaria and Ukraine (for the latter invitation letters are required). The 1995 Law on Residence and Border Crossing regulates residence, visa and border crossing procedures. Readmission agreements are in place with Austria and its other neighbouring countries, Romania, Croatian Slovenia and Bulgaria. Slovakia is currently negotiating such agreements with the Benelux countries and Germany. Border management is currently being modernized.

Police cooperation

Organized crime is active in Slovakia in the fields of drug trafficking, trafficking in humans and prostitution, racketeering, smuggling of arms, radioactive material, cultural artefacts, stolen cars and currency; violence, blackmail and extortion are used. Special units and procedures have been set up in the police and financial authorities to tackle organized crime (and drugs and stolen cars in particular) more effectively. Slovakia has signed the money laundering conventions, and domestic law criminalizes money laundering, although implementation is hampered by resource and institutional constraints. (See also separate section on the single market). Slovakia experiences no internal terrorist threat. It has signed the key terrorist conventions and has adopted appropriate legal and administrative measures to tackle terrorism.

Drugs

Slovakia is a transit country for drug trafficking, on the northern Balkan route. Significant quantities of heroin have been seized in recent years. Domestic demand is increasing sharply. Slovakia has acceded to the main international drugs conventions and is preparing a draft law on the control of drug abuse and drug precursors. The Slovak police have an anti-drugs unit and a joint drugs unit with customs as well as liaison officers in Prague, Vienna and Budapest.

Judicial cooperation

Slovakia is working to improve training and solve institutional problems in the judiciary. Slovakia has ratified the main criminal conventions (except the 1990 money laundering convention – see above). Slovakia is party to a number of Hague conventions and is beginning to develop its capacities on the civil side as well.

Current and prospective assessment

There are some important gaps still to be filled in Slovakia's legislation but for the most part the legislation is in place or in preparation. An important priority is the development of effective JHA institutions free from corruption. Important concerns are the accountability of the police and the independence of the judiciary. Some progress has been made in combating organized crime but there is still considerable work to do to develop and maintain the required degree of effectiveness. Migration and border control systems will require considerable strengthening to cope with continuing pressure.

The government has taken some steps to prepare the institutions and legislative framework for participation in the JHA process. There is a small core of officials with some experience of cooperation with EU counterparts but this will need to be developed considerably in future years.

Conclusion

Slovakia appears to have the administrative capacity and infrastructure to meet the justice and home affairs *acquis* (present and future) in the medium term. But it will have to demonstrate its commitment to introduce the necessary reforms, notably in the development of visa policy toward the NIS, border management and migration control, extradition, and combating organized crime and corruption.

3.8. External policies

Trade and international economic relations

The *acquis* in this field is made up principally of the Community's multilateral and bilateral commercial policy commitments, and its autonomous commercial defence instruments.

The Europe Agreement includes provisions in several areas requiring parties to act in accordance with WTO/GATT principles, or other relevant international obligations.

The White Paper includes no provisions in this field.

Descriptive summary

Slovakia has developed an open, trading economy and is a member of the World Trade Organization (WTO). Upon accession Slovakia would have to comply with the obligations of the plurilateral WTO agreements to which the Community is a party.

At present Slovakia does not maintain quantitative restrictions on any textile or clothing products. On accession the Community textiles policy would be extended to Slovakia; any Community restrictions still maintained at the date of accession would require adjustment by an appropriate amount to take account of Slovak accession.

Current and prospective assessment

On accession Slovakia would have to apply the Community's common customs tariff, and the external trade provisions of the common agricultural policy. The post Uruguay Round weighted average levels of most favoured nation duties for industrial products will be 3.8% for Slovakia and 3.6% for the Community.

In its relations with international organizations Slovakia should ensure that its actions and commitments respect the Europe Agreement and ensure a harmonious adoption of its future obligations as a member of the Community. In view of the interest expressed by Slovakia in mid-1996 in discussing with the Russian Federation the possibility of a free trade agreement, the EU indicated that any such arrangement should be compatible with the Europe Agreement, and with Slovakia's future obligations as a member of the EU.

On accession, Slovakia would become party to the Community's various preferential agreements. Preferential agreements between Slovakia and third countries would, in general, have to be terminated on accession.

In the area of trade in services and establishment it should be possible to resolve any remaining, significant inconsistencies between the commitments of Slovakia and the Community, although some additional liberalization may be required in Slovakia.

On accession, Slovakia would have to repeal national legislation in the field of commercial defence instruments, and EC legislation would become applicable there.

Experience from previous accessions has shown that the automatic extension of existing anti-dumping measures to new Member States prompts third countries to raise problems in terms of the compatibility of this approach with relevant WTO provisions. It has also shown that accession creates a potential for circumventing measures adopted by the Community under the commercial defence instruments. This happens when, prior to accession, substantial quantities of the products subject to measures are exported to the territory of the future Member State and, on accession, are automatically released for free circulation in the enlarged customs territory. These two problems would have to be addressed during Slovakia's pre-accession phase.

Slovakia is a member of three out of four existing regimes for the nonproliferation of weapons of mass-destruction, and is a candidate for membership of the fourth. Slovakia's list of dual-use goods and technologies largely resembles the Community control list of dual-use items. Arms export is also controlled. It is difficult to assess the extent to which export controls are effectively enforced, but Slovakia appears to have no major problems applying EC legislation in this field.

Conclusion

Slovakia is well placed to be able to meet Community requirements in this field within the next few years.

Development

The *acquis* in the development sector is made up principally of the Lomé Convention, which runs until early 2000.

Neither the Europe Agreement or the White Paper include provisions in this field.

Descriptive summary

Slovakia has no preferential trade agreements with ACP countries. However, under its GSP scheme, Slovakia grants preferential treatment in the form of reduced duties to a number of ACP countries, and grants duty free access to those ACP countries considered as least developed countries.

Slovakia has no budget for development aid.

Current and prospective assessment

On accession, Slovakia should apply its preferential trade regime to the ACP States and participate, together with the other Member States, in financing the European Development Fund (EDF), which provides financial aid under the Lomé Convention.

Applying the present Lomé trade regime should not generally be a source of difficulties for Slovakia.

Normally, new Member States accede to the Lomé Convention by means of a protocol on the date of their accession to the European Union.

Conclusion

Slovakia is well placed to be able to meet EU requirements in this field in the next few years.

Customs

The *acquis* in this sector is the Community customs code and its implementing provisions; the EC's combined nomenclature; the common customs tariff including trade preferences, tariff quotas and tariff suspensions; and other customs-related legislation outside the scope of the customs code.

The Europe Agreement covers the establishment of a free trade area with the Community and the progressive removal of customs duties on a wide range of products, according to clear timetables starting from the date of entry into force of the agreement.

The White Paper includes, in Stage I, measures to consolidate and streamline the free trade established under the Europe Agreement, including legislation compatible with the customs code, combined nomenclature, etc. Stage II concerns the adoption of the full Community legislation, with a view to joining the customs union upon accession.

Descriptive summary

On accession, the Slovak customs authorities would be required to assume all the responsibilities necessary for the protection and control of their part of the EU's external border. Besides the provisions on indirect taxation, they would be responsible for the implementation and enforcement at the external border of the Community's common commercial policy, the common agricultural policy, the common fisheries policy, etc.

Slovakia's capacity fully to apply the *acquis* presupposes the possibility to adopt and implement the Community legislation; and the existence of an adequate level of infrastructure and equipment, in particular in terms of computerization and investigation, means the establishment of an efficient customs organization with a sufficient number of qualified and motivated staff showing a high degree of integrity.

With the support of the technical assistance provided by customs programmes, the Slovak Republic has achieved almost full compatibility of its legislation with the Community's customs code and its implementing provisions. Nevertheless, important delays exist in the customs-related legislation outside the scope of the customs code.

Slovakia is undertaking a continuous process of aligning its national goods nomenclature to the Community's combined nomenclature. Presently, Slovakia is working on the preparation of an integrated tariff which will greatly facilitate the comparison of the Slovak tariff rates with the common customs tariff rates. In addition, the Slovak Republic operates a binding tariff information system similar to the one applied in the Community.

Slovakia adopted, on 1 January 1997, the new system of cumulation of origin between European countries. Slovakia became a contracting party to the EC/EFTA Common Transit Convention and to the Convention on Simplification of Formalities on 1 July 1996.

Current and prospective assessment

Slovakia would need to adapt its national procedures to the Community legislation regarding suspensive arrangements and customs procedures with economic impact. At the moment of accession, some technical transitional arrangements would be needed, notably for operations beginning before the date of accession but which are concluded after that date.

The import deposit scheme operated by Slovakia is a measure having equivalent effect to a quantitative restriction. Consequently this scheme should be abolished as soon as possible.

It will be important that the Slovak customs authorities can participate appropriately in the various computerized systems necessary for the management, in the customs union/internal market, of the customs and indirect tax provisions, as well as the computerized systems for mutual administrative assistance in customs, agricultural and indirect tax matters.

Slovakia would need on accession to dismantle customs controls at the borders with EU Member States and with other acceding countries. The resources needed for the reinforcement of the border posts along its frontiers with non-EU Member States should be taken into account in its strategic planning.

A potential for a problem exists arising from the customs union between Slovakia and the Czech Republic, in the event that these two countries do not accede simultaneously to the Community.

Conclusion

Slovakia is making a major effort to align its organization and staff to the duties that have to be carried out by a modern customs administration.

If it reinforces its efforts, particularly in relation to project management in the computerization area, Slovakia should be ready to fulfil the responsibilities of an EU customs administration within the next few years.

Common foreign and security policy

Since 1989, the foreign and security policy of Slovakia (prior to 1993, Czechoslovakia) has been reoriented towards European and Euro-Atlantic integration. Slovakia has been an active participant in the dialogue arrangements provided for under the Union's common foreign and security policy and when invited has supported EU actions within that framework.

Slovakia is a member of the UN, OSCE, Council of Europe and many other international organizations. It is an associate partner of WEU, participates in the NACC, the PfP and has made clear its desire to become a member of the WEU and NATO as soon as possible. It has sent troops to participate in IFOR/SFOR. It also participates in a number of regional organizations including CEFTA and the CEI.

There are no territorial disputes between Slovakia and any Member State of the Union. Neither does Slovakia have any territorial disputes with neighbouring associated countries. There are, however, some differences with Hungary in interpretation of their bilateral treaty and there remains a dispute with the same country over the Gabcikovo dam. This dispute has been referred to the International Court of Justice at The Hague and both parties have agreed to abide by the adjudication. Slovakia has signed with all neighbouring countries (apart from Austria) new treaties in respect of State frontiers or negotiated the succession in respect of existing

treaties. There remain some minor issues to be settled with the Czech Republic. The Slovak minority in the Czech Republic enjoys all fundamental rights and does not pose a problem.

There are good relations and close links between Slovakia and Russia: for example the military cooperation treaty of 26 August 1993 (one of 70 treaties between Slovakia and Russia) lays down the commitment 'to proceed without delay with consultations if either contracting party is concerned about a threat to its security interests'.

The Slovak Republic has a largely new and medium-sized diplomatic service which would permit it as a member of the Union to play an adequate role. It maintains 64 representations abroad and employs 556 diplomatic staff.

Slovakia supports non-proliferation of nuclear, biological and chemical weapons and is a signatory to all relevant international arms control agreements. It exercises strict control concerning the dual use of technology being a member or candidate member of all the major existing export control regimes. The Slovak armed forces, which are under democratic control, are being reorganized to meet modern requirements. The defence industrial base, which has declined significantly in recent years, continues to suffer from a number of major problems and is also in the process of re-organization.

The Slovak Government has confirmed to the Commission that it is ready and able to participate fully and actively in the common foreign and security policy.

The assessment of Slovak foreign and security policy to date leads to the expectation that as a member it could fulfil its obligations in this field.

3.9. Financial questions

Financial control

The implementation of Community policies, especially for agriculture and the Structural Funds, requires efficient management and control systems for public expenditure, with provisions to fight fraud. Approximation of legislation is moreover needed to allow the system of 'own resources' to be introduced, with satisfactory provision for accounting.

The Europe Agreement contains no specific provisions on financial control; however it provides for cooperation in audit including technical assistance from the Community as appropriate. The White Paper includes no measures in this field.

Descriptive summary

The Highest Control Office (HCO) of the Slovak Republic is an independent external body controlling the management of finances of the national budget, the management and treatment of national property, the treatment of property rights and debt-claims of the republic, etc. The HCO submits an annual report to the parliament on the results of its control activities and its opinion on the national budget. The HCO can be requested by the parliament to perform specific investigations.

The central bodies of the State administration are responsible for performing the internal financial control of the national budget in the organizations for which they are responsible. In particular, the Ministry of Finance performs such controls on all subjects connected to the national budget. Local State administration authorities perform controls over that part of the budget attributed for their use.

Various Slovak bodies are concerned with the fight against fraud, including the Central Customs Agency. National customs control is conducted from the Customs Head Office, which is responsible for the implementation of laws, international conventions, etc. and local customs control is performed by the different local customs offices. There is no independent customs internal control body, but such internal control is subordinated to the management concerned by the control action.

Specific legislation on fraud does not exist. Fraud is treated under the provisions of the Criminal Code. The Office of Financial Police of the Police Corps under the Ministry of the Interior is charged with the coordination of activities related to the disclosure of tax fraud and illegal financial transactions. This office is authorized not only to investigate suspicious financial and taxation operations but, as well, to make suggestions for amendments to existing legislation so as to better facilitate the fight against fraud.

Current and prospective assessment

The institutional structure for adequate financial control has been established and basic legislation enacted. The extent to which the legislation is being effectively implemented is difficult to assess. Further cooperation with the Slovak Authorities is needed to determine whether the HCO and the other control authorities enjoy the necessary independence from the government to carry out their duties. There is a need for improvement in existing agriculture-related financial system.

Furthermore, the financial control sector is facing the same kind of difficulties encountered by the public administration sector in general.

Conclusion

Major efforts are essential to strengthen financial control and audit functions.

Budgetary implications

The communication entitled 'Agenda 2000' sets out the overall financial framework which should accommodate the budget impact of any future enlargements in the medium term. This is to ensure that any enlargement is compatible with proposed Community policy guidelines within reasonable budget limits.

As things stand, it would be difficult, not to say premature, to attempt precise country-by-country evaluations of the budgetary implications of each of the applicants joining the Union. Exactly what the impact would be may vary considerably depending on a whole series of factors:

☐ the date on which the applicant country joins;

☐ developments in Community policies between now and then, in particular the decisions to be taken on further reform of the common agricultural policy and new guidelines for structural measures;

☐ the progress made by the applicant countries in terms of growth, increasing their competitiveness and productivity and their ability to absorb the *acquis*;

☐ the transitional measures that will come out of the negotiations.

Only a few orders of magnitude for certain budget categories and an overall estimate can be given purely as a guide.

Expenditure

If the common agricultural policy were to be reformed along the lines suggested by the Commission, once the reforms were fully up and running and in terms of just market intervention measures, Slovakia's accession would give rise to only marginal additional expenditure in relation to likely expenditure on the present 15 Member States.

As regards structural measures, the existing allocations for the Union's less prosperous Member States account for about 3 to 4% of their GNP. After a phasing-in period, the allocations for the new countries could approach the same sort of level, which would be well within the absorption capacity of the recipients.

Application of the other internal Community policies in the new member countries would be likely to involve additional expenditure probably in excess of their relative proportion of Union GNP, since for certain policies the additional implementing costs also depend on the target population, the geographical area covered or the number of Member States involved in the coordination and harmonization measures. The GNP of Slovakia is currently about 0.2% of total Union GNP.

By contrast, Slovakia's accession should not involve significant additional expenditure as far as Union external action is concerned.

It should not be forgotten that when an applicant country joins, the Community budget will no longer have to bear the costs of grants the country was eligible for under the various pre-accession programmes, such as PHARE.

In light of the above, the estimated costs in the three areas mentioned arising from Slovakia's accession should fall within the range of, annually, ECU 1.0 to 1.3 billion from 2005 to 2006 (at constant 1997 prices).

Revenue

Assuming full application of the own resources system, the new members' contributions to the Community budget should, in terms of total GNP and VAT resources (taking account of the capping rules applying to VAT), be close to the proportion of the Union's GNP they account for, which in Slovakia's case is about 0.2%. Slovakia's portion of traditional own resources will depend on the structure of its trade flows at the time of accession.

To ensure that the own resources are established, monitored and made available in line with Community regulations, Slovakia will have to overhaul its current customs system. In addition, for the purposes of accurately calculating the GNP resource considerable improvements will have to be made to the national accounts to ensure that they are reliable, homogeneous and complete. Improving the statistics will also be essential for drawing up the VAT own resources base, which will mean bringing Slovakia's VAT system fully into line with the Community directives.

4. Administrative capacity to apply the *acquis*

The European Council in Madrid in December 1995 concluded that the harmonious integration into the EU of the Central and Eastern European applicant States would, in particular, require the adjustment of their administrative structures. This chapter examines the current state of the public administration in Slovakia, including relevant aspects of the judicial system, and assesses the current and prospective ability to carry out the functions required of it in a modern, democratic State, with a particular focus on the need to administer matters related to the *acquis*.

4.1. Administrative structures

A description of Slovak constitutional structures, their powers and responsibilities, including those of regional and local government, is given in Chapter 1.

At the central level there are 15 ministries and 10 central agencies responsible to the government. Within the central government, the Office of the Government acts as a central coordinating authority under the responsibility of the Prime Minister and two Deputy Prime Ministers.

Article 73 of the labour code regulates the rights of civil servants. There is currently no specific civil service legislation, but that, as well as a general code of conduct for public officials, is under preparation.

Appointments to many positions in the civil service at national, regional and local level, and at various levels of seniority are at least in part politically determined.

In 1995, approximately 136 000 persons were employed in the Slovak public administration. Salaries in the public sector are broadly comparable with those in the private sector.

Efforts to improve the quality of the civil service have led to the establishment of an Institute for Public Administration under the responsibility of the Ministry of the Interior.

The responsibility for European integration has been vested in the Office of the Government, with one Deputy Prime Minister being charged with the overall policy concerning integration and the other bearing the responsibility for the government's legislative programme. There are 133 officials dealing specifically with European integration and the adoption of the *acquis*. The government has indicated that it will reinforce the part of the public administration dealing with European integration by recruiting and training an additional 107 officials. It intends to establish a European Education Centre. (See also the section in the introduction concerning relations between the European Union and Slovakia).

4.2. Administrative and judicial capacity

Czechoslovakia was administered under central planning during the communist period. The communist system rejected the primacy of the rule of law and subjugated the law and the administration to the implementation of party policy. Against this background, both the administration and the rule of law itself increasingly came to be seen by the public as instruments of political control.

Considerable progress has been made since 1993. The administrative structure/framework which is in place is comparable to that found in EU countries. The tasks of the administrative units and control bodies at the central level are reasonably well defined.

There are strengths in the system. For example, the capacity of individual agencies, such as the Slovak Nuclear Authority, the Anti-Monopoly Office, the Statistics Office, and the Slovak Central Bank is generally adequate. However, there are also weaknesses, notably in relation to the structure, the scope, tasks and competence of a number of institutions which throws into question their ability to effectively execute a legislative programme from the drafting stage to the implementation and enforcement of legislation. The recent regional reorganization has created an implementation/ enforcement vacuum as responsibilities previously vested at both the central and the local level are transferred to the regional level. This has particularly affected environmental inspection and monitoring, but applies as well in other areas.

The legal basis of the civil service is not yet fully adequate, but the new law should represent a substantial improvement. On the other hand, there is little sign at the moment that in practice the political independence of the civil service will be developed.

There are many human resource problems confronting the Slovak administration. There is not a problem of under staffing. However, there is a lack of sufficiently qualified staff. Language skills are not sufficiently well developed. As yet, a comprehensive strategy for the training and retraining of civil servants has not been developed. High turnover of civil servants at all levels is a problem. It is particularly critical at the high level, given that policy-making, legal, managerial and planning capacities, essential to the accession process, are in short supply. The problem of staff turnover has been exacerbated by the level of politicization of the civil service.

Public confidence in the civil service is generally low, particularly at the regional and district level where people come into most direct contact with officials. In particular, the public at large appears to perceive widespread abuse of office by officials. A recent report from the Supreme Audit Office points to frequent abuse of public funds by ministries, with 105 inspections revealing 1 093 cases of violations of the law on public orders and other relevant legislation and petty corruption is not uncommon.

For all levels of the civil service there is an urgent need to upgrade professional capacities, reinforce ethical standards and promote a corporate sense of public service across all government departments. Language skills will have to be considerably improved in order to facilitate contacts with European institutions as well as to allow for faster and more direct access to documents relating to European integration.

The coordination capacity within the Office of Government has proved to be weak, resulting in delays in preparing key strategic documents, the related legislative programme for the approximation of legislation and the implementation of that programme. Planned reforms in the EU policy area are, by definition, untested but in principle should go a long way to dealing with these problems.

Key areas for the implementation of the acquis

The uniform application of EC law: The effective application of the acquis presupposes that the judicial authorities of Member States are able to apply the provisions of the Treaty dealing with ensuring the unity and application of the acquis, and are able to ensure the proper functioning of the single market and Community policies in general. A high quality and well trained and resourced judiciary is necessary for the application by the courts of EC law, including cases of direct effect, and cases of referral to the European Court of Justice under the terms of Article 177 of the EC Treaty.

The judicial system in Slovakia has important weaknesses, particularly concerning resources, and relevant expertise. Given this situation, the Commission has significant doubts about the ability of the system to assure the effective application of the *acquis*.

Single market: The ability of Slovakia to ensure the correct application of Community requirements in the single market, particularly concerning the free movement of goods and services, presupposes the existence of highly developed and effective, regulatory standardization, certification and supervisory authorities, able to act fully in accordance with EC rules. An analysis of these points is made in Chapter 3.1. (under 'The four freedoms').

Concerning the administrative capacity in respect of free movement of goods the situation in Slovakia is broadly adequate. However, the capacity of the Patent Office and the copyright authorities in the Ministry of Culture to implement intellectual and industrial property legislation is weak. The customs administration's ability to combat piracy has not been well demonstrated. Concerning the free movement of services the situation has positive aspects. The Slovak National Bank is responsible for banking supervision (its Banking Supervisory Authority department has 52 staff) and has coped well with the task. However, there appears to be under staffing in certain areas (there are, for example, only nine on-site banking inspectors). The ability of the Insurance Supervisory Authority to monitor and control the industry is weak.

In order to meet EC requirements in this area there is a need for enhanced training in a variety of specialized areas. The implementation and enforcement of legislation would benefit from the creation of an independent securities commission.

Competition: As explained in Chapter 3.1. (under 'Competition') enforcement of competition law requires the establishment of anti-trust and State aid monitoring authorities, and that the judicial system, the public administration and the relevant economic operators have a sufficient understanding of competition law and policy.

In Slovakia the central authority is the Anti-monopoly Office, which has 40 members of staff; this is adequate. The level of expertise is not fully sufficient. The ability effectively to implement EC requirements in this field will require further investment in human resource development (especially concerning training in EC law), the definition of the competencies of the Anti-monopoly office, and improvements in transparency. Expertise in the State aids area needs improvement.

Telecommunications: In order to formulate and implement the many liberalization regulations contained in the *acquis* in this field it is necessary to have a regulatory and policy-making body that is effectively separated from any operating company.

The Telecommunications Office and the Regional Telecommunications Offices are part of the State administration. The administrative capacity will need to be strengthened.

Indirect taxation: The effective administration of the indirect taxation *acquis* presupposes structures capable of implementing the EC legislation concerning the harmonization of valued-added tax and excise duties in an environment in which fiscal controls at internal EU frontiers have been abolished; and the excise system is based on the tax warehouses, duty being payable at the local rate in the Member State at the time the goods are consumed. This requires a highly developed and well trained and resourced service, with a high degree of integrity.

In Slovakia the relevant authority is the ministry of Finance (a central ministry, six regional offices, and local tax offices additionally). The total number of staff is about 5 000. Due to a large turnover of staff, resulting partly from trained staff being recruited by the private sector, it is difficult to assess the capacities of existing staff. In order to ensure the effective administration of the *acquis* in this area it will be necessary to consolidate and improve the overall professional standards of the staff, including training measures and improvements in pay.

Agriculture: The administrative requirements in the agricultural area primarily concern veterinary and phytosanitary control, to protect public health and ensure the free movement of agricultural goods; and the ability to administer the mechanisms and requirements of the CAP, including high standards of financial control and official statistics. These points are dealt with in Chapter 3.4. (under 'Agriculture'); general standards in the statistical field are examined in Chapter 3.3. (under 'Statistics').

Concerning the administrative capacity in respect of veterinary and phytosanitary controls, Slovakia traditionally had a well established infrastructure for veterinary control and inspection, both at the borders and internally. Administrative changes which have taken place in the veterinary structure at the regional level could, however, lead to difficulties in implementation and enforcement. Numbers of staff in the food and veterinary inspectorates are not currently available to the Commission. Concerning the administration of general CAP requirements, some administrative adjustments will be required. There are 280 staff in the central Ministry of Agriculture.

In order to meet EC requirements in this area, improvements will be necessary, despite some good progress.

Transport: The application of the EC internal market and competition requirements to the transport sector, the development of relevant infrastructure products, and other aspects of the transport acquis will present administrative challenges to new Member States.

The responsible government authority in Slovakia is the Ministry of Transport. The number of staff is currently not available to the Commission. Following the separation with the Czech Republic, Slovakia has not been able to establish an appropriate administrative structure which is fully capable of carrying out all the required functions. This is of particular concern as it relates to safety controls, as well as the control of standards.

Employment and social policy: A central administrative requirement in respect of the acquis in this area is adequate inspection capacity, particularly concerning health and safety at work.

In Slovakia the labour inspectorate (approximately 180 staff) requires considerable reinforcement of staff resources and expertise.

Regional policy and cohesion: The main administrative requirements in this area are the existence of appropriate and effective administrative bodies at regional level, and in particular a high degree of competence and integrity in the administration of Community funds.

In Slovakia the Office for the Strategy of Developing the Society, Science and Technology is the State body charged with ensuring the proper implementation of regional initiatives, although its role is mainly consultative. The number of staff employed is not currently available to the

Commission. The operational and organizational arrangements for regional policy in Slovakia are deficient. The situation concerning financial control is not satisfactory (see the section, below, on 'Financial control'). The effective administration of the acquis in this area will require significant efforts to create an appropriate institutional, administrative and budgetary framework.

Environment: Since EC environmental policy involves the integration of environmental protection into EC sectoral policies the administrative requirement is potentially very wide, affecting many bodies not normally associated with environmental protection. However, the main responsibility lies with environment ministries and various subsidiary bodies.

In Slovakia, the Environment Ministry employs 291 staff. Monitoring is carried out by the Slovak Environmental Agency and sectoral authorities, enforcement by the Ministry and State Inspectorate. These arrangements are not yet adequate since competencies are not clearly defined. The effective administration of the acquis in this area will require greater financial and human resources.

Consumer protection: In this area, the effective administration of the acquis requires the allocation of overall responsibility to a specific State body through which the formulation, implementation and enforcement of consumer policy and consumer protection legislation can be undertaken.

In Slovakia, the governmental Department of Internal Trade and Consumer Protection has been given full authority to develop and implement consumer protection policy. As regards non-governmental consumer bodies in Slovakia an already strong and independent consumer movement has developed. There remains confusion about the exact scope and objectives of consumer policy. This in part explains difficulties in the effective enforcement of consumer laws; however, other factors which need to be addressed include a lack of expert staff, organizational deficits, and a lack of sensitivity to consumer questions among the judiciary.

Justice and home affairs: Oversight of justice and home affairs questions falls to the justice and interior ministries. The administrative structures need to be able to deal effectively with asylum and migration questions, border management, police cooperation and judicial cooperation. There is an overriding need for sufficient and properly trained staff with a high degree of integrity.

In Slovakia, the justice and interior ministries are adequately staffed. The capacity to handle asylum and migration questions is not yet assured, since staff in the Migration Office are inexperienced. Border management systems are outdated and need considerable reinforcing, but improvements are planned. Specialized police units have been established to combat organized crime, but cooperation with other countries is poor. The administration of the judiciary is being reformed, but cooperation with other countries should be improved. The effective administration of the *acquis* will require improvements to police accountability, the independence of the judiciary, and the strengthening of the institutional framework.

Customs: Applying the *acquis* in this area requires an adequate level of infrastructure and equipment, including computerization and investigation resources, and the establishment of an efficient customs organization with a sufficient number of qualified and motivated staff showing a high degree of integrity.

In Slovakia the customs service employs about 5 000 staff. Due to a high turnover of staff, it is difficult to estimate their efficiency, and therefore the adequacy of staffing levels. The effective administration of the *acquis* in this area will require the retention of experienced and qualified staff, and computerization of the customs administration.

Financial control: The protection of the Community's financial interests requires the develop-ment of anti-fraud services, training of specialized staff (investigators, magistrates) and the reinforcement of systems of specific cooperation. The implementation of Community policies, especially for agriculture and the Structural Funds, requires efficient management and control systems for public expenditure, with provisions to fight fraud. Administratively it is essential to have a clear separation between external and internal control. Police and judicial authorities need to be able to effectively handle complex transnational financial crime (including fraud, corruption and money laundering) which could affect the Community's financial interests.

In Slovakia the main external control body is the Highest Control Office with 250 staff. The effective administration of the *acquis* in this area will require major efforts to strengthen the institutional structures.

4.3. General evaluation

Provided Slovakia undertakes comprehensive and significantly enhanced reform efforts in this area it could be envisaged that the necessary administrative structures would be in place, in the medium term, to effectively administer the *acquis*.

Concerning the judicial capacity to effectively apply Community law, a definite evaluation at this stage is difficult.

C. Summary and conclusion

Slovakia submitted its application for membership of the European Union on 27 June 1995. Its request is part of the historic process of ending the division of Europe and consolidating the establishment of democracy across the continent.

In accordance with the provisions of Article O of the Treaty, the Commission has, at the request of the Council, prepared an opinion on Slovakia's request for membership.

Slovakia's preparation for membership is going forward notably on the basis of the Europe Agreement which entered into force in February 1995. Implementation of the White Paper of May 1995 on the internal market, another essential element of the pre-accession strategy, is going ahead on the basis of a plan agreed by the government. The government has put in place the necessary mechanisms to coordinate its policies for European integration.

In preparing its opinion, the Commission has applied the criteria established at the Copenhagen European Council in June 1993. The conclusions of this Council stated that those candidate countries of Central and Eastern Europe who wish to do so shall become members of the Union if they meet the following conditions:

☐ stability of institutions guaranteeing democracy, the rule of law, human rights and respect for and protection of minorities;

☐ the existence of a functioning market economy, as well as the ability to cope with competitive pressures and market forces within the Union;

☐ the ability to take on the obligations of membership, including adherence to the aims of political, economic and monetary union.

A judgment on these three groups of criteria – political, economic, and the ability to take on the *acquis* – depends also on the capacity of a country's administrative and legal systems to put into effect the principles of democracy and the market economy and to apply and enforce the *acquis* in practice.

The method followed in preparing these opinions has been to analyse the situation in each candidate country, looking forward to the medium-term prospects, and taking into account progress accomplished and reforms already under way. For the political criteria, the Commission has analysed the current situation, going beyond a formal account of the institutions to examine how democracy and the rule of law operate in practice.

1. Political criteria

Slovakia's situation presents a number of problems in respect of the criteria defined by the European Council in Copenhagen.

The operation of Slovakia's institutions is characterized by the fact that the government does not sufficiently respect the powers devolved by the Constitution to other bodies and that it too often disregards the rights of the opposition. The constant tension between the government and the President of the Republic is one example of this. Similarly, the way in which the government recently ignored the decisions of the Constitutional Court and the Central Referendum Commission on the occasion of the vote on 23 and 24 May 1997 directly threatened the stability of the institutions. The frequent refusal to involve the opposition in the operation of the institutions, particularly in respect of parliamentary control, reinforces this tendency.

In this context, the use made by the government of the police and the secret services is worrying. Substantial efforts need to be made to ensure fuller independence of the judicial system, so that it can function in satisfactory conditions. The fight against corruption needs to be pursued with greater effectiveness.

Apart from this the treatment of the Hungarian minority, which still lacks the benefit of a law on use of minority languages, even though the Slovak authorities had undertaken to adopt one, as envisaged by the constitution, needs to be improved. The situation of the Roma similarly needs attention from the authorities.

In the light of these elements, although the institutional framework defined by the Slovak Constitution responds to the needs of a parliamentary democracy where elections are free and fair, nevertheless the situation is unsatisfactory both in terms of the stability of the institutions and of the extent to which they are rooted in political life. Despite recommendations made by the European Union in a number of démarches and declarations, there has been no noticeable improvement.

2. Economic criteria

After a fall in GNP of nearly 25% between 1989 and 1993 Slovakia has seen positive growth since 1994 which in 1995 and 1996 reached high levels (6.8% in 1995, 6.9% in 1996), while inflation has fallen (5.4% in 1996). This has, however, been accompanied by an increase in budget deficits and in particular by a worsening of external accounts.

Slovakia has 5.4 million inhabitants and its GDP per capita is 41% of the EU average. The agricultural sector employs nearly 10% of the working population, and produces 6% of gross value added. Trade relations with the EU have grown considerably since 1989 and now represent 36% of Slovakia's imports and 41% of its exports.

On the basis of this analysis, the Commission's judgment as to Slovakia's ability to meet the economic criteria established at Copenhagen is as follows:

Slovakia has introduced most of the reforms necessary to establish a market economy. The price system has been liberalized and allocation decisions are decentralized by the advanced privatization process. Nevertheless, a restrictive Price Law was introduced in 1996, and the draft Enterprise Revitalization Act would be a major step back from market mechanisms. The financial sector needs to be reinforced, and progress is needed in the regulation of the bankruptcy process and capital markets.

Slovakia should be able to cope with competitive pressure and market forces within the Union in the medium term, but this would require more transparent and market-based policies. For a number of years, the economy has grown rapidly, with low inflation. The country has low wage costs and a skilled labour force. However, enterprise restructuring has been slow, which is gradually undermining economic growth and external balance. The low level of foreign direct investment reflects these structural problems, which need to be tackled swiftly and in a transparent way.

3. Capacity to take on the obligations of membership

Slovakia's ability to take on the *acquis* has been evaluated according to a number of indicators:

☐ the obligations set out in the Europe Agreement, particularly those relating to the right of establishment, national treatment, free circulation of goods, intellectual property and public procurement;

☐ implementation of the measures set out in the White Paper as essential for establishing the single market;

☐ progressive transposition of the other parts of the *acquis*.

Slovakia has, for the most part, met its obligations under the Europe Agreement and mostly according to the timetable for implementation set out in it. The agreement has operated in a satisfactory manner, but it has not been possible to resolve all the problems which have arisen in relation to both the democratic functioning of the institutions and commercial matters. In particular, the introduction by Slovakia of a system of import deposits is not in accordance with the agreement. Slovakia has achieved a satisfactory rate of transposition of the rules and directives identified in the White Paper.

Significant progress has been achieved on transposing legislation related to key areas of the single market such as company law, banking, free movement of capital and taxation, even if further work is needed to achieve full alignment with EC rules. More substantial efforts are needed to apply the *acquis* in the medium term on standards and certification, industrial and intellectual property, competition, public procurement and insurance.

Notwithstanding the efforts which have been made, the progress made in transposing legislation still needs to be accompanied by concrete measures of implementation as well as establishment of an effective administrative underpinning. Slovakia has a number of instruments which operate correctly, but substantial efforts are still needed in some sectors, notably public procurement, industrial and intellectual property and standardization.

As for the other parts of the *acquis*, provided it continues its efforts, Slovakia should not have particular difficulty in applying it in the medium term in the following fields: education, training and youth; research and technological development; audio-visual; small and medium enterprises; consumer protection; international trade relations; and development.

By contrast, Slovakia will need to make substantial efforts in order to apply the *acquis* in the fields of telecommunications and customs.

The integration of Slovak industry in the European market could face difficulties to proceed satisfactorily over the medium term. This will require diversification away from heavy industries and more effective restructuring of enterprises.

For the environment, very important efforts will be needed, including massive investment and strengthening of administrative capacity for enforcement of legislation. Full compliance with the *acquis* could only be expected in the long to very long term.

Slovakia has made efforts towards applying the *acquis* in the field of transport. But further progress is needed on road freight transport and the railway sector, without which it would be hard for Slovakia to meet the obligations of accession. Only if the situation improves is the transport sector unlikely to pose major problems. Slovakia needs to make the necessary effort, in collaboration with the international financial institutions, to integrate itself into the European transport network and to achieve establishment of the TENs which are important elements in the effective functioning of the single market.

Slovakia still has substantial work to do to align its employment and social affairs standards on those of the EU. Progress is needed in particular on labour law, health and safety at work and the labour inspectorate, which does not currently have the autonomy necessary to fulfil its role properly.

As for regional policy and cohesion Slovakia needs to pay more attention to existing regional disparities, and also to establish the necessary financial controls, in order to apply Community rules and in due course utilize the Structural Funds.

In agriculture, provided there is progress on veterinary and phytosanitary controls, on strengthening of the structures needed to apply CAP and on re-structuring the agri-food sector, accession in the medium term should not cause significant problems for Slovakia in implementing the CAP in an appropriate manner.

As for energy, work is still needed on operation of monopolies, price fixing, access to networks and State intervention in the solid fuel sector. Slovakia has a nuclear power station at Bohunice which produces nearly 50% of the country's electricity; and is constructing a new power station at Mochovce. It must in the medium term modernize two of the units at Bohunice to bring them up to internationally accepted safety standards; and must take the appropriate measures to close the units which cannot be modernized. A long-term solution needs to be found for nuclear waste.

On the basis of the analysis of its capacity to apply the acquis it is not yet possible to be sure when Slovakia could become able to take and implement the measures necessary to remove the controls at borders between Slovakia and Member States of the Union and to replace them at the Union's external border.

Slovakia's participation in the third stage of economic and monetary union, which implies coordination of economic policy and the complete liberalization of capital movements, could present some difficulties given the incompatibility of the rules governing the central bank with those of the EU, and also the need to restructure the banking sector. It is premature to judge whether Slovakia will be in a position by the time of its accession, to participate in the Euro area. That will depend on how far the success of its structural transformation enables it to achieve and sustain permanently the convergence criteria. These are, however, not a condition for membership.

Slovakia should be able to apply the *acquis* on justice and home affairs in the medium term, though particular attention needs to be given to frontier controls, visa policy and the fight against organized crime. Progress in this sector will also depend on respect for fundamental democratic rights.

Slovakia should be able to fulfil its obligations in respect of the common foreign and security policy.

Since 1989 Slovakia has strengthened its relations with its neighbours and settled almost all its disputes with them.

4. Administrative and legal capacity

If Slovakia undertakes substantial efforts to reform its administration, the necessary structures could be in place in the medium term to apply the *acquis* effectively.

The capacity of the judicial system to ensure correct and uniform application of Community law is important, particularly for achievement of the single market. In current circumstances it is difficult to judge Slovakia's progress in this field.

Conclusion

In the light of these considerations, the Commission concludes that Slovakia does not fulfil in a satisfying manner the political conditions set out by the European Council in Copenhagen, because of the instability of Slovakia's institutions, their lack of rootedness in political life and the shortcomings in the functioning of its democracy.

This situation is so much more regrettable since Slovakia could satisfy the economic criteria in the medium term and is firmly committed to take on the *acquis*, particularly concerning the internal market, even if further progress is still required to ensure the effective application of the *acquis*.

In the light of these considerations, the Commission considers that negotiations for accession to European Union should be opened with Slovakia as soon as it has made the necessary progress in satisfying the conditions of membership defined by the European Council in Copenhagen.

The reinforced pre-accession strategy will help Slovakia to prepare itself better to meet the obligations of membership, and to take action to improve the shortcomings identified in the opinions. The Commission will present a report no later than the end of 1998 on the progress Slovakia has achieved.

Annex

Composition of Parliament

Political party		Seats	%
Movement for a Democratic Slovakia	HZDS	61	40.6
Association of Slovak Workers	ZRS	13	8.7
Slovak National Party	SNS	9	6.0
Party of the Democratic Left	SDL	18	12.0
Christian Democratic Movement	KDH	17	11.3
Hungarian Coalition		17	11.3
Democratic Union of Slovakia	DU	15	10.0

Single market: White Paper measures

This table is based on information provided by the Slovak authorities and confirmed by them as correct as at the end of June 1997. It does not indicate the Commission's agreement with their analysis. The table includes directives and regulations cited in the White Paper which total 899. These have been listed in accordance with the categorization used in the White Paper and in relation to the policy areas covered. The table shows the number of measures for which the Slovak Republic authorities have notified the existence of adopted legislation having some degree of compatibility with the corresponding White Paper measures.

White Paper chapters		Directives		Regulations		Total
		Stage I	Stage II/III	Stage I	Stage II/III	
1. Free movement of capital	Slovak Republic	**2**	**1**	**0**	**0**	**3**
	Number of White Paper measures	3	1	0	0	4
2. Free movement and safety of industrial products	Slovak Republic	**50**	**100**	**3**	**1**	**154**
	Number of White Paper measures	56	104	4	1	165
3. Competition	Slovak Republic	**3**	**0**	**1**	**0**	**4**
	Number of White Paper measures	3	0	1	0	4
4. Social policy and action	Slovak Republic	**12**	**14**	**0**	**2**	**28**
	Number of White Paper measures	12	15	0	2	29
5. Agriculture	Slovak Republic	**93**	**44**	**53**	**2**	**192**
	Number of White Paper measures	93	46	62	2	203
6. Transport	Slovak Republic	**19**	**14**	**6**	**13**	**52**
	Number of White Paper measures	19	15	8	13	55
7. Audio-visual	Slovak Republic	**1**	**0**	**0**	**0**	**1**
	Number of White Paper measures	1	0	0	0	1
8. Environment	Slovak Republic	**16**	**7**	**6**	**0**	**29**
	Number of White Paper measures	31	7	7	0	45
9. Telecommunication	Slovak Republic	**9**	**2**	**0**	**0**	**11**
	Number of White Paper measures	9	7	0	0	16
10. Direct taxation	Slovak Republic	**2**	**2**	**0**	**0**	**4**
	Number of White Paper measures	2	2	0	0	4
11. Free movement of goods	Slovak Republic	**0**	**0**	**0**	**0**	**0**
	Number of White Paper measures	0	0	0	0	0
12. Public procurement	Slovak Republic	**5**	**1**	**0**	**0**	**6**
	Number of White Paper measures	5	1	0	0	6
13. Financial services	Slovak Republic	**12**	**6**	**0**	**0**	**18**
	Number of White Paper measures	13	8	0	0	21
14. Protection of personal data	Slovak Republic	**0**	**0**	**0**	**0**	**0**
	Number of White Paper measures	0	2	0	0	2
15. Company law	Slovak Republic	**2**	**3**	**0**	**0**	**5**
	Number of White Paper measures	2	3	0	1	6
16. Accountancy	Slovak Republic	**3**	**2**	**0**	**0**	**5**
	Number of White Paper measures	3	2	0	0	5
17. Civil law	Slovak Republic	**1**	**0**	**0**	**0**	**1**
	Number of White Paper measures	1	1	0	0	2
18. Mutual recognition of professional qualifications	Slovak Republic	**2**	**16**	**0**	**0**	**18**
	Number of White Paper measures	2	16	0	0	18
19. Intellectual property	Slovak Republic	**5**	**2**	**0**	**0**	**7**
	Number of White Paper measures	5	3	0	3	11
20. Energy	Slovak Republic	**3**	**2**	**3**	**0**	**8**
	Number of White Paper measures	10	2	3	0	15
21. Customs law	Slovak Republic	**0**	**0**	**14**	**38**	**52**
	Number of White Paper measures	2	1	14	184	201
22. Indirect taxation	Slovak Republic	**15**	**34**	**0**	**6**	**55**
	Number of White Paper measures	15	54	0	6	75
23. Customer protection	Slovak Republic	**8**	**3**	**0**	**0**	**11**
	Number of White Paper measures	8	3	0	0	11
Total	Slovak Republic	**263**	**253**	**86**	**62**	**664**
	Number of White Paper measures	295	293	99	212	899

Statistical data

If not explicitly stated otherwise, data contained in this annex are collected from the 'Statistical Office of the Slovak Republic (ŠTATISTICK´Y ÚRAD SLOVENSKEJ REPUBLIKY) with whom Eurostat and Member States' statistical offices have been cooperating for several years in the framework of the PHARE programme. Regular data collection and dissemination are part of this cooperation process with the aim of enabling the application of EU laws and practices in statistics. The data presented below have been compiled as far as possible using EU definitions and standards which in some cases differ from national practices. This may occasionally give rise to differences between the data presented here and those shown elsewhere in the opinion, which are generally based on the individual applicant countries' updated replies to the questionnaire sent to them in April 1996. The exact compatibility with EU standards on statistics and thus the comparability with EU figures can still not be guaranteed, particularly those statistics that have not been supplied through Eurostat, but have been delivered directly by the countries concerned. Wherever available, methodological notes are given describing content and particularities of statistical data presented in this annex. Data correspond to the information available as of May 1997.

Basic data

	1990	1992	1993	1994	1995
		1 000 hectares			
Total area			4 904.0	4 904.0	
Population (end of the period)		in 1 000			
– Total		5 314.0	5 336.0	5 356.0	5 368.0
– Females			2 737.4	2 747.6	2 753.8
– Males			2 598.6	2 608.4	2 6514.2
		per 1 km²			
Population density		108.0	108.0	109.0	109.0
		in % of total population			
Urban population		57.2	56.9	57.0	57.0
		per 1 000 of population			
Death rate		10.1	8.9	9.6	9.8
Birth rate		14.1	13.8	12.4	11.5
Income and GDP per capita		European currency unit			
– Average monthly wage and salary per employee					
– GDP per capita					2 467.0
Structure of production: share of branch GVA		in % of total gross value-added			
– agriculture	7.4				6.3
– industry	49.9				31.9
– construction	9.2				5.1
– services	33.5				57.2

Share of branch GVA in 1990

Share of branch GVA in 1995

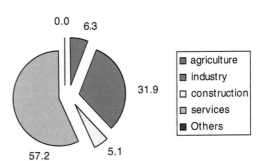

National accounts

	1990	1991	1992	1993	1994	1995
	in millions of national currency					
Gross domestic product (current pric.)	278 020	319 689	332 257	369 900	441 300	518 000
	in billions of ECU					
Gross domestic product (current pric.)				10.3	11.6	13.3
	in purchasing power standard per capita					
Gross domestic product				5 870.5	6 384.3	7 117.4
	% change over the previous year					
Gross domestic product		− 14.6	− 6.5	− 3.9	4.9	6.8
Final consumption expenditure		− 25.6	− 1.7	− 1.7	− 3.4	2.9
– of households and NPISH		− 28.3	− 6.4	− 1.8	0.0	3.4
– of general government		− 17.8	9.9	− 2.2	− 10.5	1.6
Gross fixed capital formation		− 25.2	− 4.5	− 4.2	− 5.1	5.8
Exports of goods and services		33.4	47.5	− 0.2	14.1	3.5
Imports of goods and services		− 14.7	47.1	− 0.7	− 3.5	9.6
	in % of gross domestic product					
Final consumption expenditure	75.8	71.8	78.0	78.2	72.3	69.2
– of households and NPISH	53.9	51.2	49.5	53.2	50.4	49.0
– of general government	21.9	20.6	25.6	25.0	21.8	20.2
Gross fixed capital formation	34.3	28.3	32.9	32.4	29.5	29.2
Exports of goods and services	26.5	46.3	70.3	61.7	65.2	63.2
Imports of goods and services	35.6	49.3	74.3	67.2	59.7	61.4

PIB (% change of the previous year)

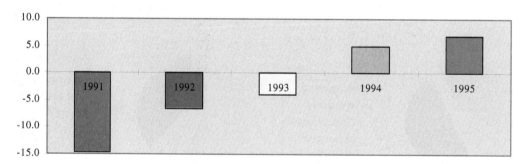

Main economic indicators

	1990	1991	1992	1993	1994	1995	1996
	% change over the previous year						
Inflation rate	10.4	61.2	10.0	23.2	13.4	9.9	5.8
	previous year = 100						
Industrial production volume indices				96.2	104.8	108.3	102.5
Gross agricultural production volume indices				92.0	102.6	100.1	
Unemployment rate (ILO methodology)	in % of labour force						
– total				12.2	13.3	12.8	10.9
– less than 25 years					26.2	23.5	19.8
– 25 years and more					10.6	10.5	9.1
	in billions of USD						
Gross foreign debt				1 317	1 916		
Balance of payments	in millions of USD						
– Exports of goods				5 447	6 691	8 579	8 830
– Imports of goods				– 6 379	– 6 632	– 8 807	– 10 936
– Trade balance				– 932	59	– 228	– 2 106
– Services, net				267	657	540	7
– Income, net				– 38	– 119	– 14	– 45
– Current account balance				– 601	665	391	– 1 941
– Capital and final account (exclude reserves)				548	129	993	2 098
– Reserve assets				– 55	– 1 290	– 1 579	– 237

Inflation rate: % change of yearly average over the previous year – all items index (data are based on national CPIs which are not strictly comparable).

Industrial production volume indices: Industrial production covers mining and quarrying, manufacturing and electricity, gas and water supply (according to the NACE classification sections C,D,E). The data cover total industrial production including estimates for enterprises of up to 24 employees and for tradesmen. Indices for branches, however, cover only enterprises with 25 or more employees.

Gross agricultural production volume indices: The gross agricultural output has been calculated on the basis of the gross turnover at current prices. Agricultural output index is recalculated to constant prices of 1989.

Unemployment rate (by ILO methodology): % of the unemployed in labour force. This rate is derived from LFSS (labor force survey) observing the following ILO definitions and recommendations where:
Labor force – employed and unemployed persons in the sense of the ILO definitions stated below.
The employed – all persons aged 15+, who during the reference period worked at least one hour for wage or salary or other remuneration as employees, entrepreneurs, members of cooperatives or contributing family workers. Members of armed forces and women on child-care leave are included.
The unemployed – all persons aged 15+, who concurrently meet all three conditions of the ILO definition for being classified as the unemployed: (i) have no work, (ii) are actively seeking a job and (iii) are ready to take up a job within a fortnight.
In the Slovak Republic, for practical reasons, the quarters do not correspond to calendar ones, but they are shifted one month ahead. The persons on compulsory military service are excluded from the employed. On the other hand, women on additional child-care leave are included.

Gross foreign debt: Debt is extracted form the OECD's external debt statistics.

Balance of payments: Data is derived from IMF database, their comparability with respective EU statistics can not be guaranteed, but balance of payments is compiled mainly in accordance with IMF standards. Balance in trade of goods in accordance with balance of payments principles. Exports and imports are both in f.o.b. values. Net income includes direct, portfolio and other investment income, compensation of employees. Current account balance by definition of IMF fifth manual, capital transfers are excluded. Reserve assets: it means changes in reserve assets during the year; (+) signifies an increase, (–) a decrease in reserve assets.

Foreign trade

	1992	1993	1994	1995	1996
Imports and exports (current prices)	in millions of USD				
– Imports		6 337	6 611	8 770	10 936
– Exports		5 450	6 691	8 579	8 831
– Balance of trade		– 887	80	– 191	– 2 105
External trade volume indices	previous year = 100				
– Imports					
– Exports					
Structure of import by SITC (current prices)	in % of total import				
– (0+1) food and live animals, beverage and tobacco	5.2	8.8	8.2	8.0	7.1
– 2 crude materials, inedible	7.0	5.2	5.3	6.0	4.9
– 3 mineral fuels and lubricants		20.9	19.3	17.5	16.9
– 4 animal and vegetable oils, etc.	0.1	0.2	0.3	0.2	0.2
– 5 chemicals and related products	9.8	11.3	13.2	13.6	11.5
– 6 manufactured goods classified chiefly by material		15.1	16.8	17.8	15.4
– 7 machinery and transport equipment	33.0	29.3	27.7	28.9	35.1
– 8 miscellaneous manufactured articles	8.3	9.0	9.1	8.0	8.9
– 9 goods not elsewhere classified		0.2			
Structure of export by SITC (current prices)	in % of total export				
– (0+1) food and live animals, beverage and tobacco	7.9	6.4	5.5	5.9	4.5
– 2 crude materials, inedible	5.5	4.9	5.1	5.1	4.5
– 3 mineral fuels and lubricants		4.9	4.6	4.2	4.9
– 4 animal and vegetable oils, etc.	0.1	0.1	0.1	0.1	0.1
– 5 chemicals and related products	11.2	12.0	12.9	13.2	12.4
– 6 manufactured goods classified chiefly by material		38.8	39.4	40.4	38.3
– 7 machinery and transport equipment	17.4	19.4	19.0	18.8	23.2
– 8 miscellaneous manufactured articles	15.2	13.4	13.4	12.2	12.1
– 9 goods not elsewhere classified		0.1			
External trade price indices	previous year = 100				
– Imports					
– Exports					

Imports and exports (current prices) and structure of external trade by SITC (current prices): Trade data exclude direct re-exports, trade in services and trade with customs free zones as well as licenses, know-how and patents. The data are based upon the special trade system. Trade classifications – the Slovak Republic is using the commodity classification according to the combined nomenclature. Imports are recorded on FOB basis and are captured with the date the commodities are released into circulation in the country. Exports are recorded on FOB basis and are captured with the date on which the commodities cross the state border. The customs statistics are utilized for monitoring of foreign trade data. Eurostat has converted national currencies to the US dollar by applying the International Monetary Fund annual average exchange rates.

Foreign trade

		1992		1993		1994		1995		1996
Structure of imports by main countries (current prices)		in % of total imports								
– first partner	RU	35.0	CZ	35.9	CZ	29.6	CZ	27.7	CZ	24.5
– second partner	D	21.0	RU	19.5	RU	18.0	RU	16.6	RU	17.7
– third partner	A	10.2	D	11.4	D	13.4	D	14.3	D	14.5
– fourth partner	I	5.7	A	6.2	A	5.8	A	5.1	A	4.7
– fifth partner	PL	3.2	I	3.0	I	4.4	I	4.6	I	5.9
– others		24.9		24.0		28.8		31.7		32.6
Structure of exports by main countries (current prices)		in % of total exports								
– first partner	D	24.4	CZ	42.4	CZ	37.4	CZ	34.5	CZ	31.0
– second partner	RU	16.8	D	15.2	D	17.1	D	18.4	D	21.2
– third partner	A	7.4	A	5.0	A	5.3	A	4.9	A	6.0
– fourth partner	HU	6.9	RU	4.7	I	4.3	I	4.7	I	4.9
– fifth partner	I	5.5	HU	4.5	RU	4.1	PL	4.3	PL	4.8
– others		39.0		28.2		31.8		33.3		32.0

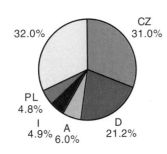

Structure of export by main partners in 1996

CZ 31.0%
32.0%
PL 4.8%
I 4.9%
A 6.0%
D 21.2%

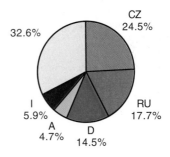

Structure of import by main partners in 1996

32.6%
CZ 24.5%
I 5.9%
A 4.7%
D 14.5%
RU 17.7%

A	Austria
CZ	Czech Republic
D	Germany
HU	Hungary

I	Italy
PL	Poland
RU	Russian Federation

Social indicators

	1991	1992	1993	1994	1995
Population on 1 January	thousand				
	5 271.71	5 295.88	5 314.15	5 336.50	5 356.00
Proportion of population by age 1 January 1995	in % of total population				
0-14					22.90
15-24					16.70
25-44					29.90
45-64					19.70
65 +					10.80
	total number				
Live births	78 570	74 640	73 256	66 370	
Deaths	54 621	53 423	52 707	51 386	
Infant deaths					
– Less than 1 year	1 041	939	779	743	
– Still birth	381	357	327	274	
Marriages	32 714	33 880	30 771	28 155	
Divorces	7 893	8 057	8 143	8 666	
	per 1000 of population				
Crude marriage rate	6.20	6.40	5.80	5.30	5.10
Crude divorce rate	1.49	1.52	1.53	1.60	1.70
Natural growth rate	4.50	4.00	3.90	2.80	
Net migration rate	0.04	– 0.50	0.30	0.90	
Total population growth rate	4.60	3.40	4.20	3.70	
Total fertility rate	2.05	1.98	1.92	1.66	
Infant mortality rate	13.25	12.58	10.63	11.19	11.00
Late foetal mortality rate	4.83	4.76	4.44	4.11	
Life expectancy	at birth				
– Males		66.60	68.40	68.30	68.40
– Females		75.40	76.70	76.50	76.30
Life expectancy	at 65 years				
– Males					12.70
– Females					16.10

Net migration: Including statistical discrepancies.

Labour market

	1993	1994	1995	1996
Economic activity rate (ILO methodology)	% of population aged +15			
	62.1	61.7	61.6	61.4
Average employment	in thousand			
	2 012	1 977	2 020	2 036
Unemployment rate by age (ILO methodology)	in % of labour force			
– total	12.2	13.3	12.8	10.9
– less than 25 years		26.2	23.5	19.8
– 25 years and more		10.6	10.5	9.1
Registered unemployment (end of period)	in % of economically active population			
	14.4	14.8	13.1	12.8
Average paid employment indices by NACE classes	previous year = 100			
– Agriculture, hunting, forestry and fishing	85.1	87.7	93.2	91.8
– Mining and quarrying	81.0	88.6	95.6	103.9
– Manufacturing		94.3	101.4	98.0
– Production and distribution of electricity, gas and water		99.6	98.1	101.2
– Construction		87.3	95.2	97.4
– Transport, storage and communication		96.7	97.5	98.2
Monthly nominal wages and salaries indices by NACE classes				
– Agriculture, hunting, forestry and fishing	109.8	113.9	112.4	112.7
– Mining and quarrying	118.8	113.9	116.8	108.8
– Manufacturing	119.8	118.3	116.2	114.4
– Production and distribution of electricity, gas and water	129.3	112.9	113.0	110.1
– Construction	119.8	117.5	115.2	116.5
– Transport, storage and communication	123.5	121.3	116.7	113.8
Monthly wages and salaries indices				
– nominal	118.4	117.0	114.3	113.3
– real	96.4	103.0	104.4	107.2

Economic activity rate (ILO methodology): – % of labour force in the total population aged 15+. This rate is derivated from LFSS (labour force survey) observing the following ILO definitions and recommendations where:

Labour force – employed and unemployed persons in the sense of the ILO definitions stated below.

The employed – all persons aged 15+, who during the reference period worked at least one hour for a wage or salary or other remuneration as employees, entrepreneurs, members of cooperatives or contributing family workers. Members of armed forces and women on child-care leave are included.

The unemployed – all persons aged 15+, who concurrently meet all three conditions of the ILO definition for being classified as the unemployed: (i) have no work, (ii) are actively seeking a job and (iii) are ready to take up a job within a fortnight.

In the Slovak Republic, LFSS excludes persons on compulsory military service and persons living in non-private households (so-called institutional population).

Unemployment rate (by ILO methodology): – % of the unemployed in labour force. This rate is derived from LFSS (labour force survey) observing the following ILO definitions and recommendations (see ILO definitions above).

In the Slovak Republic, for practical reasons, the quarters do not correspond to calendar ones, but they are shifted one month ahead. The persons on compulsory military service are excluded from the employed. On the other hand, women on additional child-care leave are included.

Average employment and average paid employment indices by NACE classes: The data for entrepreneurial sphere cover all organizations (including organizations of up to 24 employees and estimates for tradesmen and their employees). The data cover also all budgetary, subsidized organizations and persons with secondary jobs are included. Armed forces, apprentices, employees on child-care and additional child-care leaves are excluded.

Registered unemployment (end of period): – Registered unemployment as % of unemployed registered in civil economically active population, based on labour force sample survey (LFSS). The unemployment rate was calculated for 1994 on economically active persons covered by the balance of the labour force for 1992 year. Since 1995 it has been based on economically active persons (LFSS) for the previous year and numbers of unemployed registered by labour offices.

Monthly wages and salaries indices:– Monthly real wages and salaries indices are derived from gross nominal wages and salaries indices divided by cost of living index. – The data for entrepreneurial sphere cover organizations of up to 24 employees and estimates for tradesmen, including estimation for workers employed by tradesman (less entrepreneurial incomes). The data also cover all budgetary, subsidized organizations and persons with secondary jobs are included. Armed forces, apprentices, employees on child-care and additional child-care leaves are excluded.

Financial sector

	1990	1991	1992	1993	1994	1995	1996
Monetary aggregates				billions of US dollars			
– Monetary aggregate M1				3.50	4.12	5.02	5.45
– Quasi money				4.12	5.48	7.06	7.62
Total reserves (gold excluded, end of period)				millions of US dollars			
				416	1 691	3 364	3 419
Average short-therm interest rates				% per annum			
– lending rate				14.41	14.56	15.64	13.22
– deposit rate				8.02	9.32	9.01	6.18
Official discount rate (end of period)					12.00	9.75	8.80
USD exchange rates				1 USD = ... SKK			
– Average of period				30.770	32.045	29.713	30.654
– End of period				33.202	31.277	29.569	31.895
ECU exchange rates				1 ECU = ... SKK			
– Average of period				36.032	38.118	38.865	40.097
– End of period				37.043	38.472	38.861	39.964

Public finance (Government budget): Data are not available.

Monetary aggregates: Money (M1) includes demand deposits and currency outside banks. Quasi money (QM) includes time, savings and foreign currency deposits. Eurostat has converted national currencies to the US dollar by applying the International Monetary Fund annual end of period exchange rates.

Total reserves (gold excluded, end of period): The statistics on official foreign reserves are extracted from the IMF's monthly international financial Statistics (IFS). Total reserves (gold excluded) are defined as the sum of central bank holdings of foreign currencies and other (gross) claims on non-residents; this definition excludes claims on residents denominated in foreign currency. According to the definition; official foreign reserves are calculated at market exchange rates and prices in force at the end of the period under consideration. Total reserves (gold excluded) published in IFS may differ from the figures published by the national authorities. Some factors contributing to possible differences are the valuation of the reserve position in the fund, and a different treatment of claims in non-convertible currencies.

Average short-term interest rates: Data are extracted from the IMF's monthly international financial statistics (IFS). Average short-term lending and deposit rates relate to period averages. Lending rates generally consist of the average interest rate charged on loans granted by reporting banks. Deposit rates relate to average demand and time deposit rates or average time deposit rates. These rates may not be strictly comparable across countries to the extent the representative value of the reporting banks and the weighting schemes vary.

USD exchange rates: International Monetary Fund exchange rates as present in the publication: *Statistiques Financières Internationales.*

Inflation (12 months changes)

Percentage change of the CPIs with the current month compared with the corresponding month of the previous year (t/t-12)

	Jan.	Feb.	Mar.	Apr.	May	Jun.	Jul.	Aug.	Sep.	Oct.	Nov.	Dec.
1993	17.6	19.4	20.3	21.6	22.0	23.6	23.9	26.0	27.1	26.3	25.6	25.0
1994	16.4	15.2	14.7	13.9	13.9	13.9	13.6	12.3	12.2	12.1	11.7	11.6
1995	11.7	11.5	11.3	11.3	11.0	10.6	10.9	9.8	8.8	7.9	7.5	7.2
1996	6.5	6.1	6.1	6.0	6.2	6.3	5.5	5.6	5.1	5.3	5.3	5.4

Inflation (% change of CPI)

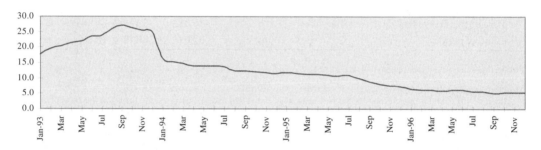

Inflation (12 months changes): Inflation rates (12 months changes) are percentage changes of the CPIs with the current month compared with the corresponding month of the previous year. Inflation rates are based on national CPIs which are not strictly comparable between candidate countries or with those based on EU HICPs (different methods, concepts, practices in the calculation of CPIs). Data are calculated from CPIs supplied by national statistical institutes.

Industry

	1993	1994	1995	1996
Structure of GDP by economic activities (NACE, current prices)	in % of gross domestic product			
— Mining and quarrying	1.0	0.9	1.0	1.0
— Manufacturing	24.6	24.3	23.3	21.3
— Production and distribution of electricity, gas and water	3.6	3.5	4.2	4.0
Industrial production volume indices by NACE classes	previous year = 100			
— Total	96.2	104.9	108.3	102.5
— Mining and quarrying	79.9	96.7	98.5	106.4
— Manufacturing	88.0	101.5	108.7	102.9
— Production and distribution of electricity, gas and water	121.0	115.9	97.5	105.1

	1993 Q1	1993 Q2	1993 Q3	1993 Q4
Industrial production volume indices by NACE classes	corresponding period of the previous year = 100			
— Total		91.0	89.0	90.0
— Mining and quarrying		97.0	92.0	91.0
— Manufacturing		81.0	82.0	86.0
— Production and distribution of electricity, gas and water		102.0	90.0	90.0

	1994 Q1	1994 Q2	1994 Q3	1994 Q4
Industrial production volume indices by NACE classes	corresponding period of the previous year = 100			
— Total	102.0	105.7	107.8	107.0
— Mining and quarrying	99.0	93.4	106.9	99.5
— Manufacturing	99.0	102.7	102.3	101.8
— Production and distribution of electricity, gas and water	115.0	110.1	120.0	117.0

	1995 Q1	1995 Q2	1995 Q3	1995 Q4
Industrial production volume indices by NACE classes	corresponding period of the previous year = 100			
— Total	105.7	109.4	109.5	108.5
— Mining and quarrying	78.8	103.2	102.2	111.6
— Manufacturing	106.7	107.7	109.0	111.4
— Production and distribution of electricity, gas and water	95.7	95.9	100.3	98.3

	1996 Q1	1996 Q2	1996 Q3	1996 Q4
Industrial production volume indices by NACE classes	corresponding period of the previous year = 100			
— Total	107.1	99.8	101.9	101.6
— Mining and quarrying	112.0	105.8	106.9	102.1
— Manufacturing	106.4	100.7	103.1	101.9
— Production and distribution of electricity, gas and water	115.9	99.9	105.8	98.3

Structure of GDP by economic activities (NACE, current prices): The structure of GDP by economic activities (NACE) is calculated at factor costs. Data for selected kind of activity are expressed by added value indicator. In 'C' and 'E' for enterprises with 25 and more employees only.

Industrial production volume indices by NACE classes: Industrial production covers mining and quarrying, manufacturing and electricity, gas and water supply (according to the NACE classification sections C, D, E). The data cover total industrial production including estimates for enterprises of up to 24 employees and for tradesmen. Indices for branches, however, cover only enterprises with 25 or more employees.

Infrastructure

	1991	1992	1993	1994	1995
	in km per 1 000 km²				
Railway network	75	75	75	75	75
Railway transport	in million tonnes or passenger km				
– freight transport			14 304	12 236	13 674
– passenger transport			4 569	4 548	4 110
	in 1 000 of population				
Number of telephone subscribers	247.0	256.6	267.5	284.0	301.0
	inhabitants				
Number of inhabitants per passenger car	5.8	5.6	5.3	5.4	5.3

Agriculture

	1992	1993	1994	1995	1996
Land area by land-use categories	in 1 000 ha				
– Total	4 904	4 904	4 904	4 904	4 904
– agricultural land	2 447	2 446	2 446	2 446	
– forest	1 990	1 991	1 992	1 992	
– arable land	1 509	1 486	1 483	1 483	1 479
– permanent meadows and pastures	810	831	835	835	839
Agricultural land by legal status	in % of agricultural land				
– State enterprise		22.5	22.3		
– cooperatives		69.5	69.2		
– others		8.0	8.5		

	1992	1993	1994	1995	1996
Share of GDP	in % of gross domestic product				
– Agriculture, hunting, forestry and fishing (NACE A + B)		6.6	6.6	5.6	5.2
	previous year = 100				
Gross agricultural production volume indices		92.0	102.6	100.1	102.0
Main crops by area	in 1 000 ha				
– cereals of which:	808.6	844.9	873.8	856.8	813.6
– wheat	354.4	398.0	442.9	437.8	417.5
– potatoes	51.0	47.0	41.0	41.0	41.0
– sugar beet	45.0	33.0	34.0	35.0	43.0
– fodder beet	7.0	7.0	7.0	7.0	7.0
Main crops by yield	in 100 kg/ha				
– cereals of which:	44.2	37.3	42.3	40.7	41.6
– wheat	47.9	38.4	48.4	44.3	42.5
– potatoes	128.0	182.0	96.3	106.7	
– sugar beet	294.7	338.7	331.9	336.9	
– fodder beet	379.7	436.2	382.1	409.1	

	1992	1993	1994	1995	1996
Sales or procurement of animal for slaughter	in 1 000 tonnes of live weight				
– pigs	235.1	212.2	205.4	202.2	210.2
– cattle	172.0	170.4	122.1	108.3	110.6
– poultry		54.0	59.2	67.8	67.9
Livestock breeding intensity (end of period)	heads per 1 000 ha of agricultural land				
– cattle		411	379	384	369
– of which: cows		160	149	147	139
– sheep		170	164	177	173
	heads per 1 000 ha of arable land				
– pigs		1 473	1 380	1 400	1 350
– of which: sows		112	107	109	

Structure of GDP by economic activities (NACE, current prices): The structure of GDP by economic activities (NACE) is calculated at factor costs. Data for selected kind of activity are expressed by added value indicator.

Gross agricultural production volume indices: The gross agricultural output has been calculated on the basis of the gross turnover at current prices. Agricultural output index is recalculated to constant prices of 1989.

Sales or procurement of animals for slaughter: The data refer to the sales of principal products of agriculture.

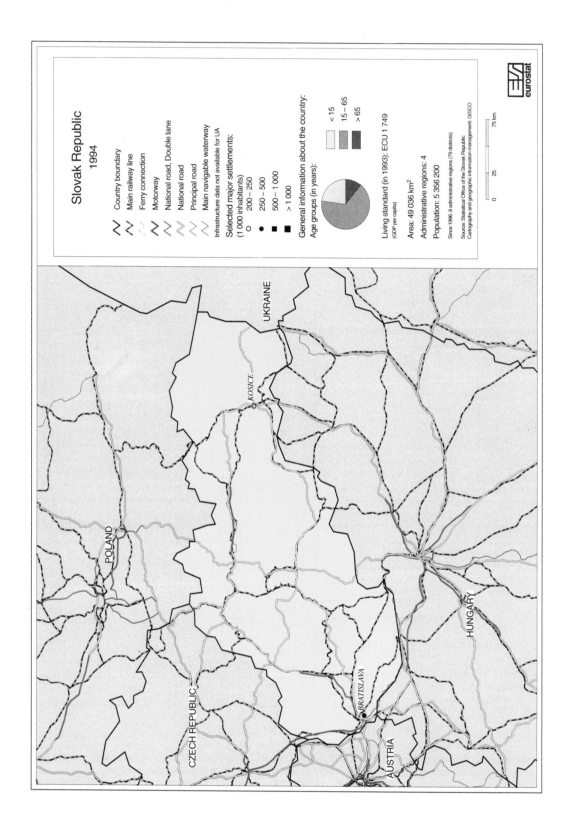

Slovak Republic
1994

Country boundary
Main railway line
Ferry connection
Motorway
National road, Double lane
National road
Principal road
Main navigable waterway
Infrastructure data not available for UA

Selected major settlements:
(1 000 inhabitants)

○ 200 – 250
● 250 – 500
■ 500 – 1 000
■ > 1 000

General information about the country:
Age groups (in years):

< 15
15 – 65
> 65

Living standard (in 1993): ECU 1 749
(GDP per capita)

Area: 49 036 km²

Administrative regions: 4

Population: 5 356 200

Source: 1996: 8 administrative regions (79 districts)
Since 1996: Statistical Office of the Slovak Republic.
Cartography and geographic information management: GISCO

UKRAINE

KOŠICE

POLAND

CZECH REPUBLIC

BRATISLAVA

AUSTRIA

HUNGARY

0   25   75 km

eurostat

98

European Commission

**Commission opinion on Slovakia's application for membership
of the European Union**

Supplement 9/97 to the Bulletin of the European Union

Luxembourg: Office for Official Publications of the European Communities

1997 – 98 pp. – 17.6 x 25 cm

ISBN 92-828-1248-0

Price (excluding VAT) in Luxembourg: ECU 7